Tom —

A book of Southern humor to a reconstructed Yankee — To help him keep his sense of humor as keen as it is on July first — 1986

Love —
Jean & Thacker

CAN I JUST DO IT TILL I NEED GLASSES?

And Other Lies Grown-ups Told You

LUDLOWPORCH

FOREWORD BY LEWIS GRIZZARD

Peachtree Publishers, Ltd.

Published by
PEACHTREE PUBLISHERS, LTD.
494 Armour Circle, N.E.
Atlanta, Georgia 30324

Copyright © 1985 Ludlow Porch

Manufactured in the United States of America

First printing

Library of Congress Catalog Number 85-61976

ISBN 0-931948-81-9

To my uncles, who single-handedly

won World War II

O. T. Hanson
U.S. Marine Corps

S. D. Kidd, Jr.
U.S. Navy

Harry J. Kidd
U.S. Army

J. M. Kidd
U.S. Army

W. P. Kidd
U.S. Army

Special Thanks

To Teresa Ward for her many hours of help;

To all the boys I grew up with, whose antics made the writing of this book necessary;

And to town character Art Leo, without whose help this book was written.

Contents

Ludlow Porch

Foreword

I GO WAY BACK with Ludlow Porch, back to his days as a nine-to-five insurance adjustor. He was pretty funny in those days, but he didn't get many laughs. I mean, a man whose house just burned to the ground and whose new Mercedes, which was parked in the driveway, now looks like a toasted marshmallow isn't exactly the best audience for a comedian.

So since Ludlow's best material was going to waste, I stole it and didn't give him credit. You can do that to a stepbrother.

Then one day *Sports Illustrated* did an article on trivia and featured Ludlow, who was an expert on the subject because he'd never done anything very significant. Next thing you know, he's on an Atlanta radio call-in show and so enamors the audience that he lands a full-time job with the station.

The rest is history: Ludlow has become the most

successful radio talk-show host in the South, has written four books and is now using his own material. I'm not happy about it, but his fans are laughing their underdrawers off.

It's not the first time he's done something like this to me. In fact, he's crossed me more times than the road in front of his house.

When I got married for the second or third time (I forget which), we were in a bit of a hurry. Like, it was Saturday afternoon about four and we wanted to be married before the sun went down. I was not at that time on a first-name basis with any preachers, so I called Ludlow and asked for help.

"No problem," he said. "Be at my house in two hours and I'll have everything arranged." Being a friend of long standing, he even offered to pick up the tickets for our honeymoon trip — an Amtrak tour of sunny Florida. What a buddy.

After the wedding, he rushed us to the train station where he handed me an envelope that supposedly held the tickets. When the conductor interrupted our marital bliss five hours later to ask for tickets, however, I discovered that the envelope was empty. What a prankster.

As soon as we picked up our luggage where we'd been thrown off the train, I called Ludlow — called him every name in the book. "I'm sure you think that's funny," I said, "but on your honeymoon night it ain't funny worth a damn."

"Well," he said with absolute calm, "if you don't think that's funny, how about this one: That fellow who married you this afternoon isn't really a preacher. He pumps gas at the Amoco station on Roosevelt Highway." And then he hung up.

For years I've been waiting for the chance to get even, and when he asked me to write a foreword for this book, I thought my time had finally come. But the truth is that no one can stay mad at Ludlow for very long, not even when he deserves it.

The Good Lord created Ludlow Porch in a moment of light heart, set him loose on an unsuspecting world and very likely sat back and had Himself a good laugh. If He hasn't lost His sense of humor, He's probably laughing yet.

The rest of us certainly are.

— **Lewis Grizzard**

1

Even President Roosevelt Wore Glasses

I WAS TAUGHT growing up that a lie was a lie. There was no such thing as a little white lie and no such thing as a fib. A lie was just a bald-faced lie.

And in my pre-school mind, there was no question about what would happen if you told lies. I knew the story of Pinocchio and how his nose grew longer with each lie he told. I knew that Jesus was always listening and would be sad if I told a lie.

Lying was so bad that kids didn't even say the word in front of grown-ups. We said, "Johnny is telling a story." We said that rather than saying, "Johnny is lying through his crooked little teeth."

I was constantly reminded that a lie was something not to be taken lightly. My grandmother, while looking very solemn, would often say, "If you call your brother or sister a fool or a liar, you are in danger of hell fire." I didn't know all the ins and outs of hell at that time, but even then I knew there was no appeal once you got there. The ball game was over.

I would try to comfort my grandmother and myself by saying, "Don't be upset, Mama, I'm an only child. Besides, I don't have to worry because I don't have a brother or a sister."

She would wrinkle her brow and say, "All men are our brothers." What I thought was a perfect loophole had been slammed shut in my face.

There was also historical precedent for telling the truth. I had learned early on that George Washington never told a lie, and it was obvious to me that Gene Autry would rather kill his horse than tell a lie. Finally it became clear and simple to me: Good people told the truth; evil, hell-bound heathens told lies.

It therefore came as somewhat of a shock to me to find out that grown-ups told lies all the time.

I will say in their defense that the lies they told me were ones they thought would make me a better person or at least keep me from harm's way.

The lie that was told most often was a common one used on all Southern children at one time or another. Any time I was bad or the least bit unruly, I was told, "If you don't stop that, I'm going to wear you out!" I heard it so much that the threat eventually lost its meaning. It lost its meaning, that is, until one day it dawned on me that wearing me out would be one hell of a horrible thing.

I was about five or six at the time, and although I had never seen a person worn out, I had seen tennis shoes that were worn out. They were dirty and ragged and had holes in their bottoms. Even at that tender age, I realized how they got that way — by receiving months and months of abuse. They were walked on, thrown in the corner wet and generally abused in every possible way.

I also had seen cars that were worn out. Their windows were smashed, their hoods were up and they were on blocks, alone and abandoned. When you're six years old, you don't want to end up on blocks, alone and abandoned. From then on I paid a lot more attention when someone threatened to wear me out.

Looking back, it seems that most of the lies grown-ups told were intended to keep me in line. That most certainly was the purpose of the Soap Sally lie. Soap Sally, for the uninformed, was the Southern version of the Bogey Man.

She was an evil old woman who closely resembled the witch in "Snow White." She walked around looking for bad children, and when she found one she kidnapped him, took him back to her shack and made soap out of him. At least that's what grown-ups said.

When I was seven, my friend Fleming moved away. It came as a shock, because I didn't know he was moving. He was there one day and gone the next. I was convinced that Fleming had fallen victim to the dreaded Soap Sally. Actually, it didn't bother me that much, because Fleming deserved pretty much whatever he got. It was, however, a matter of curiosity to me, and I remember sitting in the bathtub and picking up the soap and whispering to it, "Fleming, is that you?"

Some years later, I ran into Fleming and was reasonably relieved to see that he was still alive and had not gone down somebody's drain in the form of soap bubbles.

Although I never saw Soap Sally, it never occurred to me that she was a lie. If she was invented to keep little boys like me in line, I know of at least one case where it worked. But, of course, no lie was as effective at discouraging us from doing things we shouldn't as that wonderful, wonderful lie about Santa Claus.

"Good boys get presents. Bad boys get switches," I was warned.

"He knows when you are sleeping, he knows when you're awake," we were told in song.

"If you aren't a good boy, Santa knows," all grown-ups said.

I must have been a perfect target for the Santa Claus set-up, because my family made up a special story just for me. They told me that one year when my Uncle Simpson was a little boy, he was so bad that Santa brought him the promised bundle of switches. I bought the story, even though I knew my Uncle Simpson to be a kind, loving man, who was a successful banker as well as a city councilman and a much loved man in the community.

It seemed strange that I knew kids my age who

were so mean their dogs didn't even like them, yet they always got presents at Christmas time. I could only assume that in his young life, my Uncle Simpson had been one bad dude. Either way, I couldn't take the chance, so I was a perfect angel for weeks before Christmas.

Years later, when we were wise to Soap Sally and the Santa Claus scam, grown-ups still stuck together with lies designed to keep us in line. This was particularly true when it came to the subject of (in a whisper, please) masturbation. I say this because the same lies were told in all families and in all neighborhoods. And from the things we were told about masturbation, I assumed that grown-ups were convinced that it was evil and, if not stopped, it could cause the end of western civilization as we knew it.

Almost universally, teen-age boys were told that "pullin your puddin" would cause pimples. I must say that this particular threat didn't bother us much. We all knew that God had given the world Noxzema for just such occurrences.

Some of the other effects, however, were not so easily taken care of. It was said to be common scientific knowledge that excessive masturbation would cause hair to grow in your palm. I could only imagine the shame that could follow you through a lifetime if you were walking the streets with a hairy palm.

Everyone would know that you were a degenerate — girls would know, the preacher would know and, God forbid, your mama would know. Could even a mother love a hairy-palmed son?

If the pimples and hairy palms were not enough to keep our pants buttoned, we were told that excessive masturbation would cause blindness. My heart went out to the blind people of the world, even though I figured they had had a few very happy years. When I was eleven, somebody told me about a man who had been blind since he was three. My only comment was, "Wow!"

There was a time in my early teens when I worried constantly about waking up some morning with a hairy palm, a bad complexion and a seeing-eye dog at my side. But not even fear of blindness kept me from indulging. I always remembered the little boy who, when warned by his mother that such activity could leave him blind, said, "Well, can I just do it till I need glasses?"

If masturbation was really all that bad, I reasoned, how come I'd never heard President Roosevelt talk about it on the radio? And why had Brother Boswell never railed against it by name in his Sunday morning sermons? In fact, didn't both of them wear glasses on occasion?

I don't guess all the lies we were told did any harm, and it is impossible to resent them when you realize that their origins were in love and that they were meant to help us grow up to be better people. I'm sure that even today these same lies are circulating among young boys and that the sale of Noxzema has held steady throughout the years.

2

Does the Forecast Call for Thunder?

MY CHILDHOOD WAS full of myths, which are lies that even grown-ups believe. I've often wondered how some of those old wives' tales got started and how they evolved into the status of truth.

I grew up holding cats in contempt because of one of these myths. If there was a new baby in the house, it was absolutely critical that the baby never be left alone with the cat. Everyone knew that the cat would get in the crib, suck out the baby's breath and kill the child. That was considered an absolute fact during my childhood. I have known many cases of cats being given away when a new baby came home.

It also was common knowledge to me and my peers that if you ate fish and drank milk at the same meal you would get sick and die. There was no known antidote. Death was always swift and sure.

Ludlow Porch

Every Friday at Central Park Grammar School, fish and milk were served in the lunchroom. But every child there knew it was poison, so it was never eaten.

Occasionally we would get a new student from the North, and you could hear someone tell him, "Don't eat that. You'll be dead before you hit the floor. Old Lady Williams is a Nazi spy and she's trying to kill us all." Someone else would point out that the principal ate his fish and drank his milk and didn't die. He must be in on it, too, we figured. My God, those Nazis will stop at nothing!

Oftentimes the myths we believed were more dangerous than the actuality. When I was about eight, my grandmother sent me to the henhouse to gather eggs. The last thing she said to me as I went out the back door was, "Don't disturb the hens on the nest. Just reach under them very gently and get the eggs."

I said, "Yesem."

About halfway to the henhouse, I realized what she had said. She wanted me to reach my hand *under* the chickens without knowing for sure what was there. It was apparent that she had never heard of the dreaded chicken snake. I, on the other hand, had often heard tales of that deadly, poisonous reptile that crawled under sitting chickens, ate the eggs and waited for unsuspecting eight-year-olds.

I had to get those eggs, but I also knew that there was no way on earth I was going to stick my hand under those hens. I attempted to shoo them off the nest, but they clucked at me in a very menacing manner. I was almost as afraid of setting hens as I was of snakes.

I was frustrated and furious. Those dumb hens were going to get me in trouble with my grandmother.

I finally decided that my only option was to kill the hens and the snakes, hide the bodies and take the eggs to the house like nothing had happened. A rock. I'd kill them with a rock. No, a rock wouldn't work. I might miss and be attacked by the chickens and the snakes simultaneously.

Out of the corner of my eye, I spotted a tree limb that was about ten feet long. I picked it up and found out it was too heavy and long to swing like a baseball bat. Then I remembered seeing a picture show about the knights of the Round Table, and I remembered how they held their lances with the back part in their armpits.

I positioned the limb and attacked those two poor hens. I almost beat them to death before I realized they were off the nest and, wonder of wonder, there were no snakes in it.

I gathered the eggs and took my basket to the house and into the kitchen. My grandmother said, "Good boy. Did you have any trouble?"

"No, ma'am," I answered. "What problem could I possibly have just gathering a few eggs?"

Like all little boys, I was intrigued with turtles. I can't count the magic hours I spent playing with turtles I found in the woods. I must point out, however, that I was very careful never to play with snapping turtles.

Unfortunately, I never could just look at one of those creatures and magically tell if it was a snapping turtle or not. I therefore devised a test to distinguish a friendly garden variety turtle from the dangerous and sometimes deadly snapping turtle. I would put a stick close to the turtle's mouth. If he bit it and hung on, he was a snapper; if not, he was just a garden variety turtle and OK to play with.

It wasn't that I was afraid of being bitten. After all, I had been bitten by a dog, a cat, a crawfish and, worst of all, by my friend Bobby Sorrells.

The difference was that any fool knew that when a snapping turtle bit you, he hung on and wouldn't turn loose until it thundered. The story was that you could kill him and cut his head off and he still wouldn't turn loose.

I may have been just a little boy, but even then I knew that sometimes it went for weeks without thundering.

I had a horrible mental picture of going to Sunday school and church with a snapping turtle dangling from my index finger. I could just hear the taunts of the other children: "Look at that little boy. He must be a dumb ass. He was playing with a snapping turtle." I could see myself lying in bed at night with my turtle beside me holding on for dear life. I could hear my prayers: "God bless my mother and all my family, and please, dear God, let it thunder soon."

The myths went on and on and we believed all of them. Step on a crack, break your mother's back. Intellectually, I could not see how stepping on a crack could break my mother's back. Nevertheless, I was careful not to step on a one. I loved my mama dearly and did not want to be responsible for crippling her for life.

I was also careful not to be involved when anyone was planting a tree. I was told and believed that when you planted a tree and it grew large enough to cast a shadow that would cover your grave, you would die. In my mind, only a complete fool would plant a tree.

I learned another life-saving tip from my black friend, June Bug. He told me that if I would pee down my leg before going swimming in the wash hole, I would not get cramps. I must confess that I never heeded his advice, because I felt then, just as I feel now, that I would rather have cramps and drown than pee on my ownself.

I told June Bug that and he said, "OK, but if you get a cramp and drown, don't come complaining to me."

John Willy, another black friend, looked at me with disgust in his eyes and said, "You so dumb, I don't see how you find your way home. I hope you get a cramp. I'll just stand there and say, 'Lookee yonder at that dumb-ass, soda cracker white boy, drowning 'cause he's afraid to pee down his leg.'" I said, "John Willy, if you call me a soda cracker one more time, I'm gonna hit your ass in the head with a rock." Superstition you see, can lead to a falling out among friends.

I don't guess any of these myths caused us any great harm, even though we believed them and accepted them as the gospel and lived our lives accordingly. If nothing else, they made things a little more fun and added excitement to our lives.

We also took our dreams very seriously. Today a bad dream usually means that I shouldn't have put so much pepper sauce on the greens, but there was a time in my life when I was convinced that dreams could be a warning of things to come.

These fears were based on myths that I had been told by grown-ups or, in the more bizarre cases, by a child who was older and therefore an absolute authority on such scientific nocturnal matters.

I believed from the bottom of my little ignorant heart that if you dreamed you had died, you would never wake up.

It was also scientific knowledge, at least in my family, that if you awakened a sleepwalker he would immediately drop dead. I don't know how this idea ever started, but I almost tested it one summer.

I spent a week at Camp Burt Adams, a camp for Boy Scouts. I liked all the boys there except for Al, who was a bully and took great delight in pushing smaller kids around.

One day Al threw one of my tennis shoes in the

lake and then laughed like a fool. I was heart-broken. Tennis shoes were expensive, and to say that my family was not rich would be like saying that King Tut is dead.

I knew that my mother had worked hard and long to pay for those shoes, and that big piece of cow dung thought it was funny that one of them was on the bottom of the lake. I was furious, too.

I remember lying awake that night and watching him sleep, not twenty feet away. I was thinking, You're too big for me to fight, but if you sleepwalk tonight, your ass is mine.

Needless to say, he never walked in his sleep, but if he had, I intended to wake him up and watch him drop dead at my tennis shoe-less little feet.

Looking back, I guess I was lucky. If I had tried to wake him up while he was sleepwalking, I'm sure he would have beaten me senseless. And that's no myth.

3

Anyone Ever Heard
Of a Nipple Transplant?

I DON'T KNOW if it was due to lack of money or lack of knowledge, but during my childhood, we didn't go to a doctor for every little thing. We went only during extreme sickness or for an emergency. Therefore, grown-ups had to be familiar with every known home remedy.

Funny thing about home remedies — most of them were worse than dying.

I always felt that my mother had a less than wholesome interest in my bowel habits. I believed my bodily functions should have been between me and my Creator, and my mother should not have been overly concerned. My mother, however, was convinced that total health and happiness were the result of regular bowel habits, so she was greatly concerned.

It always started the same way. She would go into the bathroom after I had left and say, "It smells awful in here."

"It's supposed to smell awful, Mama. I just went to the bathroom," I would answer.

"No, no," she would say. "You've got to have some medicine."

I would desperately argue. "Mama, it's supposed to smell bad, I promise. If you go to the bathroom and it doesn't smell bad, *then* you need medicine." But there was no changing her mind.

That night before bed, she would come at me with the calomel. I only knew two things about calomel: one, it tasted horrible, and two, it tasted horrible. I had also heard that if you took a dose and then got wet, it would make you a cripple, but I could never prove that to my mother's satisfaction.

My wonderful mother tried everything under the sun to hide the taste of the calomel. One time she put it in orange juice, and for ten years I couldn't stand the sight of orange juice.

The bouts we had over calomel were classic. She would try anything to get that mess down my throat. She would try bribery: "If you take this like a good boy, I'll get you some ice cream."

She would try to play on my sympathy: "I've worked hard all day. Please take this so we can go to bed and get some rest."

She tried the old guilt routine: "If you love me like you're supposed to, you'll take this for me."

Then she would try the method that always worked. She'd say, "OK, young man, I've had about enough of this. You take it now or I'm going to wear you out." That always worked, because my sainted mother seldom bluffed. If she told you she was going to do something, she generally delivered.

I came along in the years before penicillin and the sulfa drugs. The wonder drug of my day was Vick's Vapor Rub. No home could hope for its residents to survive the winter if the medicine cabinet did not have a large jar of Vick's.

If, God forbid, you had a chest cold, it was rubbed all over your chest. Then you put on the top to your BVDs and slept under about three blankets. It was thought that by morning your chest cold would be better, and many times it was.

If your nose was stopped up by a head cold, a big glob of Vick's was dropped into a pot of boiling water. You then were made to lean directly over the boiling water with a towel draped over your head, thus trapping the life-saving fumes under the towel, where you could breathe them and not reduce their effectiveness with any fresh air.

You were kept in that position until your knees started to buckle and it was evident to all concerned that you were only seconds away from death. They would then take the towel away, look you right in your bloodshot eyes, and say, "Now, don't you feel a lot better?"

If you knew what was good for you, you always tried to fake a smile and say, "Yes, ma'am, a lot better."

If you made any other response, you knew that you were going right back under that towel.

If you had a sore throat, you were forced to swallow a spoonful of Vick's. I remember vividly that it tasted exactly like a spoonful of forty-weight motor oil.

If, by any chance, the Vick's plan did not work, there was a last-resort cold remedy. I mean, of course, the mustard plaster.

There were two types of mustard plasters. The first was the homemade variety. My grandmother made them herself in our kitchen. I don't know what it was made of, but I remember that it was yellow and smelled bad enough to drive termites out of the house. Again you had to sleep in a wool BVD top to make this torture work.

When you woke up in the morning (*if* you woke up in the morning), the entire room smelled like you had been raising goats. I also remember that it took about three soaking, scrubbing baths before you smelled like a human being again.

The second type of mustard plaster was the one you bought at the drugstore. It was adhesive and stuck to your chest sort of like a postage stamp. It didn't smell particularly bad, and sleeping was relatively easy with it stuck to your chest. The horror of the store-bought mustard plaster, however, came with the rising sun when you had to face the certain reality that it was time for your mother to rip the mustard plaster from your cowardly, quivering chest.

Anyone Ever Heard Of a Nipple Transplant?

When she came into the room, she would say, "Time to take that nasty mustard plaster off my baby's chest."

"Do it easy," I would plead.

"The faster I take it off," she would say, "the less it will hurt. You don't have any hair on your chest, so it'll hurt for only a second." She would then take the edge of the mustard plaster between her thumb and index finger. This was my cue to squeeze my eyes shut and say a silent prayer that the Lord would help me through it. Then suddenly and without warning, the mustard plaster was savagely torn from my chest in one lightning-fast movement. The sound was like a cat being torn in two. RIPPPPPPPPP!

It was over quickly, but I remember thinking, She's torn my nipples off! I'm only seven years old and must face the rest of my life with a nippleless chest. Dear God. I can never be a lifeguard.

I was devastated. The thought of a slick-chested future loomed in front of me. Then came the inevitable question: "Now, that wasn't so bad, was it?" I was worried about being a double nipple amputee, and there she was sitting on the side of my bed smiling. I would rather have lost both legs. I knew I could get wooden legs. But I also knew that in the history of medical science, no one had ever been fitted for artificial nipples.

I can't tell you the relief I felt when I reached down and felt both nipples in place and almost normal. Raw and burning, but nonetheless in place.

Ludlow Porch

My mother and grandmother were the Dr. Kildare and Dr. Gillespie of their day. They were convinced that any malady or sickness could be cured with one record-setting bowel movement. It was to this end that I became the unwilling guinea pig for every laxative known to medical science.

They thought that if they could disguise a laxative as chocolate, I would never know the difference. They told me that Ex-Lax was just like a Hershey bar. I remember thinking, If it's just like a Hershey bar, how come you can't get it with almonds? And if it tastes so good, how come they aren't eating it?

The same was true of Feen-A-Mint. They told me it was just like a Chicklet. To this day I won't eat Chicklets because they taste like Feen-A-Mint.

Remember Carter's Little Liver Pills? I don't know what they did for your liver, but I do remember that for a BB-sized pill, they sure made you spend a lot of time in the bathroom.

Castor oil was too vile even to talk about. I'm not sure what its medical properties were, but it tasted so bad that I was sure my castor was well oiled.

Milk of Magnesia tasted so bad that my mother wouldn't even give it to me. But that didn't stop my grandmother from giving it to me once. It tasted like a mixture of sour milk and Iranian sweat. I would rather die in the gutter than ever take it again.

3 6's was supposed to cure everything from baldness to brain tumors, but mostly it turned stom-

achs. I remember watching the faces of the adults as they took a spoonful. Their mouths drew up tighter than pantyhose on Shelley Winters. I made a silent oath that if they tried to make me take it, I would hang myself first.

I guess most of the home remedies didn't hurt us, and there may have been times when they saved our lives. But there was one cure that was many times worse than the sickness: the dreaded enema. Common sense tells you that God never meant for a human being to take an enema. He is a just God, you know. He didn't even do *that* to the devil.

My bottom line about home remedies is that they were hypocritical. Everybody said, "An apple a day will keep the doctor away."

What that really meant, of course, was, "A laxative a week will make you hit your peak." Medically speaking, it was another world and one that I don't miss.

4

A Valuable Lesson: Pig Never Bluffed

IN THE THIRTIES and forties, kids had no television and, for the most part, no organized activities. We couldn't count on our parents to drive us places or to be our activity directors, because they were too busy trying to make a living. Therefore, it fell to us to entertain ourselves, and we did it with creativity and zest.

We spent many, many hours playing Hide-and-Seek. When you play Hide-and-Seek, the first thing you must do is decide who's going to be "it."

There were several ways to do this. The one we used most was to tell the littlest kid in the group that he was going to be "it" and that if he did not cheerfully agree, he would not be allowed to play. If this method didn't work, then you counted taters to settle the issue.

Counting taters was done by having all the participants stand in a circle, clench both fists and hold them in the middle of the circle. Someone then started to count the closed fists by saying, "One potato, two potato, three potato, four. Five potato, six potato, seven potato, more." When you said "more,"the fist you landed on was put behind the owner's back. Then you started counting again. The last person with a hand in the circle had to be "it."

Once you decided on who was "it," you were ready to play Hide-and-Seek. The person who was "it" closed his eyes, put his hand against a tree and started to count to five hundred by fives . . . five, ten, fifteen, twenty, twenty-five, thirty, thirty-five and so on. When he got to five hundred, he yelled, "Bushel of wheat, bushel of rye, who's not ready holler 'I.'" Anyone who wasn't ready screamed, "I!" The person who was "it" then counted to one hundred by fives. When he reached one hundred, he yelled again, but this time he said, "Bushel of wheat, bushel of clover, who's not ready, can't hide over." Hide-and-Seek was most fun if you started playing just after the sun began to go down. You played until your mama called and said it was time to come home.

I guess my favorite game was "Throw the Can." I don't think many people outside of my small-town neighborhood played this game. Whenever I talk about it, people always try to correct me by saying, "You mean *Kick* the Can."

We never played Kick the Can, and I can assure you that compared to Throw the Can, all other games came up short.

To play Throw the Can, the first thing you needed was a can with one end cut out. Small rocks were then put in the can and the end was mashed shut. This was done so the can would make noise when it was thrown. The noise was important because Throw the Can was usually played at night.

Once you had prepared the can, a large circle was drawn with chalk in the street, preferably under a street light.

The next step was to decide who was "it." Nobody wanted to be "it" in Throw the Can. It was a hard job, not much fun, and once you became "it" you could spend hours trying to get rid of that job. The decision was usually made by counting taters.

Once you determined who was "it," everybody got in the circle and one person, generally the strongest one in the crowd, threw the can as far as he could. While the poor "it" was running after the can, everybody else would run and hide. "It" brought the can back to the circle and then started to look for the other players.

The rules called for "it" to physically run down the other players and grab them and say, "One, two, three, buck." I never did know what that meant, but somehow it made the capture official.

Once a player was captured, he was brought back to the circle and left there with the can while the person who was "it" went off to make another capture. Now came the fun part. While "it" was away from the can, another player could run into the circle, throw the can again and free all the captured players to run and hide again. The poor "it" had to run after the can and start his search all over again.

This was great fun for everyone except the guy who was "it." Usually about the third time everyone was set free, the sweat-soaked "it" would yell, "I'm quitting."

A voice would answer out of the night, "No, you ain't."

"Yes, I am. This is no fair and I'm quitting."

The voice would argue, "You can't quit till you catch everybody, and if you try, I'll beat your butt."

"It" usually would answer that threat with one of his own. "If you lay one hand on me, I'm going to hit your ass in the head with a rock."

At this point in the game, one of two things would happen: either we would all quit and sit around and talk till we had to go home, or, if we had not had enough Throw the Can for one night, someone would volunteer to be "it" and the game would continue.

Foxes and Hounds was another of my favorite games. It could be played in daytime or night, but to be played properly, it had to be played in the woods.

The few rules of the game were simple. We divided up into two teams — a team of foxes and a team of hounds.

The foxes were given a head start to find a place to hide. Then the hounds went out and tried to run them down. The game was over when the last fox had been run down. Like Throw the Can, the capture was not complete until the person was grabbed and the hound said, "One, two, three, buck." Great pride was taken if you were on the winning team, and there was always shame involved in losing anything, especially Foxes and Hounds.

One of the great finishes of all times occurred in the summer of 1947. We were playing the game in Pine Grove, a wooded area near my house. We had been playing all day, and only one fox remained free. Our acknowledged leader, Pig, was the only fox not caught. I should point out here that Pig was our leader because he would do things that would shock a Mafia chieftain, and we, of course, admired him for that.

Suddenly, we heard Floyd yelling at the top of his lungs, "I found him! I found him!" We all ran in the direction of the screaming Floyd. When we got there, sure enough, Floyd had found Pig. He was about fifty feet in the air in the very top of a huge pine tree. Floyd was saying, "OK, Pig. Come on down. You're caught."

Pig said, "I ain't caught yet."

"Sure you're caught," said Floyd. "We got you treed."

"I ain't caught till you grab me and say, 'One, two, three, buck,'" answered Pig.

The boys on Pig's team were saying, "Yeah, yeah. That's right. You ain't caught old Pig yet."

The other boys were saying, "Let's go home. I'm

hungry. You know we gotcha, Pig."

Pig hollered down, "You ain't got nobody. Shut your mouth or I'll come down and kick your butt."

The threat was not taken lightly, since at one time or another Pig had kicked most of the teen-age butts in our neighborhood.

Floyd finally said, "Pig, if you don't come down and give up, I'm gonna come up after you."

"If you try to come up here," warned Pig, "I'm gonna shit on you."

"You're bluffing. I'm coming after you," said Floyd, and he started to climb up to get Pig.

Herman was jumping up and down and shouting, "Do it, Pig! Shit on his head!"

The other boys were yelling encouragement to Floyd. "Go get 'im, Floyd. Show him you ain't scared. He won't do it."

Pig stood up on the limb and started to unbuckle his belt. By that time, Herman was almost in a frenzy. He was screaming, "Do it, Pig, do it! Shit on him."

Floyd continued up the tree. Pig pulled his pants down, squatted on one limb and held on to another over his head.

Herman, still cheerleading from the ground, yelled, "Take aim, Pig. Do it! Do it!"

Pig kept looking down, moving around trying to line up his target. I remember thinking that he reminded me of a bombardier.

When Floyd reached a spot about ten feet under Pig, he learned a lesson that would stay with him for the rest of his adolescence: Pig never bluffed.

Summertime was special. It was the time when there were no great demands on our time and we could get creative with our activities. Our biggest summertime pleasure was the wash hole. In some locales, this was referred to as the old swimming hole, but for some reason we called it the wash hole. The name doesn't make any sense when you realize that we never washed there.

We took great pride in our wash hole because we had to rebuild it every summer. We would clean out the limbs and debris that had washed downstream and settled there, and we had to dam the creek up to make it deep enough to swim and dive in. It usually took several days of hard work to get everything ready for the first swim.

The whole process, of course, had to be done with complete secrecy. Swimming in the wash hole was forbidden by our parents. They gave us all kinds of reasons, including tales of huge cottonmouth snakes and snapping turtles. They reminded us of the health risk; no one knew for sure what caused polio, but the smart money said it had something to do with swimming. The city swimming pools were all closed during any polio epidemic. They even told us that we could catch scarlet fever swimming in the creek.

None of the things they told us helped, however, because we knew the *real* reason they didn't want us there: They didn't want us swimming naked. As a matter of fact, they didn't want us doing *anything* naked.

The year I was in the seventh grade, summer came early. The temperature was in the seventies and eighties almost every day, even a month before school was out. So we started going by the wash hole on our way home from school and getting it ready.

One afternoon we couldn't stand it any longer. We stripped off to the skin and jumped into the still icy water. We were having so much fun that we soon forgot how cold it was. Suddenly I heard one of my pals say, "Dear God, look!"

We all looked up to see the principal of our school, Mr. Purcell, coming through the woods. The wash hole was empty of boys in about eight seconds.

We grabbed our clothes and lit out downstream. We could hear Mr. Purcell, who wasn't up to the chase, standing at the wash hole and yelling at the top of his lungs, "I know who you are! I know who you are!"

When we were safely out of his sight, we stopped to get dressed. We weren't quite sure just how much trouble we were in. Did he really recognize us? If so, what would he do? Would he wait and make our lives a hell on earth at school, or would he tell our parents and let them do it for him?

We discussed our options.

"Let's deny being here, no matter what."

"No, that wouldn't work."

"Can you join the Army when you're twelve?"

"Doubtful."

"Suicide. That's it. We'll make a suicide pact."

"That ain't going to work. Suppose he didn't really recognize us. Then we would have killed ourselves for nothing."

"We can run away and join the circus," said David.

"Don't be a dumb ass, I answered. It's only May and the circus won't be in town till January."

We decided to go home and just wait it out.

I spent a sleepless night but, praise the Lord, nothing happened. So far, so good.

The next morning, we had been at school for only about thirty minutes when Miss Neese, our seventh grade teacher, told us that Mr. Purcell had called a special meeting for the whole school in the auditorium. I remember thinking, Dear God, he did recognize us and he's going to kill us in front of the entire student body. This was it. Twelve years old and I was not only going to die, I was going to be publicly humiliated.

I said a prayer. "Dear Heavenly Father, if you'll get me out of this, I'll never ever get naked again. I won't even get naked to take a bath." My prayer was interrupted by Mr. Purcell's voice booming from the auditorium stage. He said, "I want the boys who were swimming in the woods yesterday to come up on this stage right now."

No chance, Mr. Purcell. Not only was I not that

stupid, I also was too scared to move. I glanced around me. To my relief, none of my co-conspirators were moving either.

"I know who you are," he continued, "and if you don't come up here in five seconds, I'm going to call your names."

He's bluffing, I thought. If he knew who we were, he wouldn't have herded the whole school in here. We were safe. Thank you, Jesus. It was a bluff.

Finally, after what seemed to be an eternity, he led us in singing, "God Bless America" and the first two verses of "Jesus Loves Me" and then dismissed us.

It was a very frightening experience and one that I have never forgotten. It made such an impression on me that it was almost ten days before I went back to the wash hole. The only difference was that afterwards we always had a lookout.

Many years after the famous wash hole raid, I was talking to Mr. Purcell. I told him that my bottom had been one of those he had seen going downstream on that warm day so many years before. He said that what we had never known was that once we were out of sight, he had collapsed in laughter at the thought of little naked boys fleeing in bare-assed terror.

Marbles were my introduction to gambling. Of course, we didn't think of shooting them as doing anything wrong, and neither did our parents.

There were, of course, some parents who would not allow their sons to play "keepsies." That merely forced their sons to "slip" and play for real on the sly. No one looked down on either the children or their parents for this prohibition, and if the subject ever came up, someone just explained it away by saying, "His folks are strict church people."

I was never very good at marbles. I don't ever recall coming out of a game as a big winner, and most of the time I felt like I was furnishing marbles for the whole neighborhood.

Hope, however, does spring eternal in the human breast, and like all my friends, I ruined many a pair of jeans by grinding the red mud into the knees until even my mother's regular Saturday scrubbing could not move that stubborn Georgia clay.

When you had a lot of marbles, it was a creative challenge to transport them from place to place. You certainly couldn't carry them in your pockets; it made you look like you had mumps of the privates.

Some of the more affluent marble players had a bag with a drawstring. I never knew where they got them, but deep down I was very jealous. I still consider it the ultimate mark of a marble hustler, and if I ever get rich, I'm going to keep my marbles in one of those drawstring bags.

Poorer kids carried their marbles in an old Prince Albert smoking tobacco can. It would hold enough marbles to get you into a game, and it fit very comfortably into your hip pocket.

If you were going to a *real* marble shoot out, you carried an old sock full of marbles.

I've never quite understood the demise of marbles. One day the playgrounds and vacant lots of America were full of boys shooting marbles, and the next day they were gone.

A few years ago I went back to Central Park School on a one-man sentimental journey. It was late in the afternoon, almost twilight, and the school was locked, so I had to content myself with walking around the empty schoolyard and thinking of the hours that I spent there. The spot where we used to shoot marbles had a swing set on it. I sat down in the swing and for a brief moment I could have sworn that I could see the setting sun reflecting off an aggie. Then I could hear two steelies bouncing off each other. And just before I got up to leave, I was almost sure I heard Gerry Allen's voice saying what he had said to me so many times in the past: "Knucks down. Knucks down."

Shooting marbles, win or lose, was a great way to pass a summer day. I almost pity today's kids who don't know the thrill.

One of the absolute miracles of my youth was the start of yo-yo season.

I don't understand to this day how the season started, but one day there wasn't a yo-yo in sight and the next day they were everywhere. The schools were full of people playing with yo-yos.

Did the governor declare yo-yo season? How did everyone know it was time to start?

As with most childhood activities, we had our yo-yo champions. There were guys in my neighborhood who could make a yo-yo hesitate for a week. We all learned how to do Rock-the-Baby, Walk-the-Dog and Around-the-World.

The height of the yo-yo season came when the Filipinos came to the picture show to hold their contest. Somewhere between the Sagebrush Raiders and *Charlie Chan in Hollywood*, the lights would come on in the theater and the manager, Mr. Crowe, would come on stage with a microphone and try to get everybody quiet. Once the noise had settled to a gentle roar, he would introduce three Philippine gentlemen who had names that even their mamas couldn't pronounce. He would explain that they worked for the Duncan Yo-Yo Company, and that first they were going to give a yo-yo demonstration and then they were going to hold a contest and give prizes to the best yo-yoers in the theater.

Then Mr. Crowe would say, "And now, here he is, boys and girls, the world champion, Carlos Whatshisname." None of us had ever heard of Carlos, but that didn't make any difference. We screamed, hollered and whistled like we knew him.

Carlos would come out, take the microphone and say, "Are jew havin' fon?" And we would scream and holler even louder.

Carlos would then introduce his two associates

and describe on the microphone what they were doing. They did all the standard tricks — only they did them using one yo-yo in each hand. Then they went to the hard tricks, like Picking-Mangos-in-the-Forest, Come-Shake-Hands-with-Juan and the Volcano. They performed feats that seemed impossible.

After their demonstration, they called contestants on stage for the contest. The winner got a T-shirt that said he was a Duncan Yo-Yo champion. The runners-up got Duncan Championship yo-yos. It was a proud day in the life of the winners.

After the contest, the Filipinos all went to the lobby where they sold yo-yos for thirty-five cents. If you had another quarter, they would pull out a long switch-blade knife and cut a palm tree with your initials on the yo-yo. Of course, that meant you had sixty cents tied up in a yo-yo, but it was worth it. Where else could you get your very own heirloom for only sixty cents? I couldn't resist.

I rushed home to show my mother my new trophy. She was a lot more impressed than I had anticipated. She said, "It's absolutely beautiful. It's much, much too pretty to play with. We should put it in the cedar chest and save it."

"Save it for what?" I whined.

"Why, save it until you get grown. So you'll know how to take care of it."

"But, Mama," I said, "the only grown-ups who play with yo-yos are Filipinos."

It took about twenty minutes of big-league whining to talk her out of putting my beautiful work of art in the cedar chest. She was right, of course, because a few days later a teacher with no appreciation for art took it away from me and I never saw it again.

I've often wondered what happened to the thousands of dollars worth of valuables that teachers confiscated — yo-yos, water pistols, peashooters, flips, marbles, pocketknives. I was convinced for awhile that all teachers owned novelty shops, where they got rich selling their ill-gotten gains.

I'm sure that today teachers are not allowed to take things from kids, because it is obviously a breach of their Constitutional rights. Besides, I imagine that Dr. Spock and his crowd would insist that if you deprive a child of his possessions, he'll grow up to be gay or a drunk or maybe even a Democrat.

I tried one time to explain to some children the joys of a dirt clod battle. They looked at me like I was nuts. So did their mothers. But such battles are fond memories of my youth.

The nice thing about an honest-to-God dirt clod fight was that there were no rules. The only thing you needed was a field that had been plowed, rained on and subjected to about three days of sunshine. The results were dirt clods that came in all sizes. The best ones were hard and crusty on the outside, so they would hold together when you threw them, and soft on the inside, so they would stick to what they hit.

The best fights seemed to start by accident. One boy would lob a clod at another one, he would lob one back and so on until somebody got hit. Then the battle was on. The more people involved, the more likely you were to get hit.

The big miracle of all this is that I don't remember anyone ever getting hurt, although, Lord knows, we tried.

Battles, in general, seemed to be big with my crowd. We had acorn battles, chinaberry battles, BB-gun battles and, my favorite of all, rubber-gun battles.

Rubber guns were made by sawing a piece of wood in the general shape of a pistol. A clothespin was attached to the handle of the gun with rubber bands. The ammunition consisted of long, thin pieces of rubber, about one-half inch wide, cut from an innertube. You stretched the pieces over the barrel and down its length, opened the clothes pin, inserted the end of the tightly stretched rubber band , closed the clothespin and you were in business. The only thing you had to do to fire was to aim the pistol and mash the end of the clothespin with your palm. You could raise a blister on whomever you hit.

Red innertubes made the best ammunition. I was able to corner the market on red innertubes, because Mr. Strickland, who owned the Texaco station on Main Street, saved all his worn-out, patched innertubes for me. I was a very popular guy with the rubber-gun set. I soon learned that I could get the older boys to make me a rubber gun in trade for a red innertube. It was my first venture into capitalism.

I don't want to leave the impression that all of our childhood activities were violent. Far from it. I also ran with a literary crowd. Comic books were a big, big part of my growing up. They cost only a dime, and you could read them ten times and then trade them with a buddy for some that were new to you.

It would be impossible to list them all, but nostalgia demands mentioning my favorites — the ones that were my closest companions. This list is not in the order of their importance to me, but I think you will see that in my youth I had a wide reading interest:

Captain Marvel
Captain Marvel, Jr.
The Adventures of
   Mary Marvel
Superman
Superboy
Supergirl
Batman and Robin
Mickey Mouse
Wonder Woman
Donald Duck
Dick Tracy

Spiderman
Mandrake the Magician
Archie Andrews
Brenda Starr
Wash Tubbs
Captain Easy
The Sky Hawks
The Hawkman
The Atom
The Blue Lantern
Zorro
Little Lulu

Ludlow Porch

Blondie and Dagwood
The Captain and the
 Kids
Plastic Man
Terry and the Pirates
The Green Hornet
Don Winslow of the
 Navy
The Little King

The Lone Ranger
Red Ryder
Spy Smasher
Secret Agent X-9
G-Men
Joe Palooka
Ozark Ike
Henry

I've often thought that had I kept all the comic books I ever owned, I could have started my own store. But reading them was only half the fun. The more you had, the more leverage you had in trading.

I never liked Little Lulu, but I knew that you could trade two Little Lulus for one Captain Marvel, and I loved Captain Marvel.

You had to know the market to be effective. For example, my younger friend, Mack, loved Little Lulu, and on a good day, I could trade him a Little Lulu even-steven for a Captain Marvel or a Superman. I liked to trade with Mack because he was a sucker. Besides, his mama gave him more money for comic books than any other kid in our neighborhood.

The greatest discovery of my academic life came in the form of comic books. They were called Classic Comics, and they were exactly what the name implied: classic stories in the form of comic books. You could get *A Tale of Two Cities*, *Romeo and Juliet*,

Silas Marner, and almost any other that you needed to write a book report on. I remember thinking, This could possibly be the greatest discovery since the Fudgecicle.

Oh, the wonderfulness of it all! Just read a comic book, make a book report, get a good grade and go on off down the road safe in the knowledge that you were ten times smarter than any literature teacher who ever lived.

I think it would be a very worthwhile project if all the folks of my generation would chip in and build a monument to the person or persons who invented the Classic Comic books. We may have occasionally abused them, but they introduced us to people and places we might never have known otherwise. They broadened our world.

On, rainy days, we would have mammoth Monopoly games. We would gather on somebody's front porch and play Monopoly non-stop for six or eight hours at a time. If Monopoly didn't suit us, we would play Five Hundred Rummy until the rain stopped and we could get back to our more active playtime pursuits.

You've probably noticed that I haven't made any mention of the activities of the little girls who grew up at the same time as me. That's because I paid little attention to them. I thought that only sissies played with girls. (I soon outgrew that silly notion.) Nonetheless, I do remember some of their activities.

Jump rope was the prime game of the girls at recess. They all played it and had rhymes to go with almost everything. They would say:

"Down in the meadow where the green grass
    grows,
There sat Suzie, sweet as a rose.
She sang, she sang, she sang so sweet,
Along came Jimmy and kissed her on the cheek.

"Why, Suzie, I'd be ashamed,
Let a boy kiss you and you don't know his
    name.
How many kisses did she get?
One, two, three, four . . ."

Many more hours were spent playing hopscotch. It was almost impossible to walk down the street without seeing hopscotch courts lined off in chalk or drawn in the dirt. It must have been a great game, because even some boys played. I must say, however, that these boys were looked down on by the rest of us.

Girls also liked to play dress-up. They would put on their mothers' old clothes, including hats and high-heeled shoes, and play by the hour.

Paper dolls were also big. They could buy paper doll books at the ten-cent store or get them out of the Sunday funnies. Every Sunday, Brenda Starr included cut-outs of Brenda and Basil, complete with two changes of clothes. No boys played with paper dolls. Not even sissies.

The single biggest pastime for boys and girls was what we called Playlike. When you're eight years old and have a Southern accent, "playlike" becomes "p'like," as in, "P'like you're the bad guy and I'm Secret Agent X-9." Or, "P'like I'm a soldier and you're a German."

The possibilities were endless. You could P'like with as few as two people or as many as twenty of your friends.

You could P'like with your Flexi racer: "P'like I'm the Green Hornet, you're Kato and the Flexi is our car, the Black Beauty." Or with your bicycle: "P'like my bike is a motorcycle and I'm a policeman."

Most of our ideas for P'like came from the picture show. We would go and sit through a Saturday double feature and then come out all set to P'like.

Robin Hood, for example, was great material for P'like. Sticks became our swords, and garbage can lids became the shields used by the sheriff of Nottingham and his bunch of cutthroats.

The rules were well defined. If during the first part of the game you had been one of Robin's Merry Men, you had to be one of the bad guys for the last part. The Merry Men never did anything that was not completely honorable. The bad guys (we called them the King's Men) never did anything that was not despicable and lowdown.

The King's Men used shields (garbage can lids),

while the Merry Men were not allowed shields.

If a good guy lost or dropped his sword during a duel, the king's man was allowed to "run him through." If, on the other hand, a bad guy lost or dropped his sword, a smiling good guy would allow him to pick it up.

No mention was ever made of the lovely Maid Marion. We maintained our posture that only sissies ever got involved with girls.

Although Errol Flynn was our hero as Robin Hood, we probably would have had more respect for him had he not insisted on kissing Olivia de Havilland right square on the mouth.

We also were big Zorro fans. The only difference between playing Zorro and Robin Hood was that whoever played Zorro got to wear a mask. Nothing fancy, usually a handkerchief.

Unlike Robin, Zorro was great with a whip. Our whip was usually P'like, meaning it did not exist. We handled that by simply saying, "P'like I got a whip."

Our favorite was to simply play cowboys and Indians, or cowboys and bad guys.

We all had what we called cap busters, or toy guns. We never had caps, but we P'liked we did by yelling, "Pow! Pow!" a lot. We used old broomsticks for horses, and every Christmas we got a fresh supply of guns and holsters and occasionally a pasteboard cowboy hat.

We used the honor system to determine who had been killed. Unfortunately, the honor system did not always work.

One day my friend R.C. shot Pig. "Bang, bang! You're dead!"

Pig said, "You missed."

"Come on, Pig," said R.C. "You're cheatin'. You know you're dead. Come on, Pig, p'like you're dead."

Pig was not one to be reasoned with. "Why don't we play like your butt's a football and I'll kick it?" said Pig.

One of the great boons of my childhood was when I would fall heir to any old box or crate. When we got rid of our old icebox and got our first Frigidaire (in the early days, all refrigerators were called Frigidaires), I was given the crate it came in.

It was one of the great P'likes of all time.

It was an airplane at first, and I flew all over the world, bombing the Japanese and Germans. I strafed their troops on Saipan and Iwo Jima. I bombed them till hell wouldn't have it on Okinawa. I tore up the Burma Road while leading my squadron of Flying Tigers in attack after attack.

I also showed the Germans no mercy. I was the first fighter pilot to bomb Berlin and send Hitler scurrying for his shelter.

Through the magic of P'like, my trusty fighter plane became a submarine. I was the first naval officer to maneuver a sub into Tokyo Bay two years before General Doolittle bombed Tokyo. I shelled them from the deck of my Frigidaire crate.

When it became a tank, I led General MacArthur ashore in the Philippines. It was my trusty tank that was first to break through at Bastogne and save the GIs trapped there.

If we were involved in a hot game of Fox and Hounds, it became the world's best hiding place.

There's just no doubt about it: A Frigidaire crate is the world's best P'like.

Sticks were also good things to P'like with. In the flash of a second, they could become a toy, a pistol, a knife, a bow and arrow, a magic wand or, if the stick was long enough, even a horse.

A stick could also be used to P'like doctors. If your friend had been wounded in a gunfight, you simply took a small stick and rubbed it over the wound while you said, "Fix, fix, fix, fix." Then, as if by magic, your wounded playmate was restored to the flower of health. Sticks could even heal gunshot wounds to the heart and the forehead.

If you grew up without P'likes in your life, you missed a lot. Because if you just stop and think about it, most of the wonderment of our childhood came from a P'like of one kind or another.

Santa Claus was a P'like, and what would our childhoods have been without that most wonderful of all fat men?

The Tooth Fairy was a P'like that actually left money. You didn't have to earn it or even be good to get it. You just saved the tooth and put it under your pillow, and in the morning there it was — cold hard cash.

And don't forget the Easter Bunny, a truly delicious P'like that left you goodies and at the same time taught you valuable lessons about Jesus.

Growing up is a risky business. There're responsibilities, debts and obligations, sicknesses and the racing hands of the clock. But the only part of growing up that really bothers me is, the older you get, the fewer P'likes there are in the world.

5

Brooksie Was Really
A Mummy's Boy

ONE OF THE most vivid memories of my childhood is sissies. I'm not talking about today's gays. I
can't tell gay from Renee Richards and probably
never will be able to, but I can spot a sissy a hundred yards away in a thick fog.

The sissies of my childhood had many things in
common. For one, they never seemed to get dirty. I
guess that was because they didn't play any of the
rough-and-tumble games that the rest of us enjoyed
so much. A sissy thought he was having a big time
if he was standing around watching the girls play
kickball. There ain't no way on earth to get dirty
watching somebody else play.

Another thing they had in common is that all of
their mothers added an *ie* to their first names. If
the sissy's name was Norman, his mama called him
Normie. Chuck became Chuckie. And Wayne
became Waynie.

All sissies also carried handkerchiefs, even when they didn't have colds.

Their bicycles, which always looked brand-new, invariably had little sissy horns on them. And I never understood why, but sissies never took the fenders off their bicycles. Maybe they never understood why we did.

They never wore jeans or levis to school, only dress pants and pressed shirts.

They all took piano lessons. Now, it's OK to take piano lessons, but what made the sissies stand out was that they didn't mind the practicing. Sissies always called their mamas, "Mother."

They never got GI or flat-top haircuts. Their hair was always neatly combed and smelled of Vitalis.

They always had their homework done. Now I know that's a wonderful thing, but when I was ten it really ticked me off.

I guess the thing that really bothered me most about sissies, though, was that girls seemed to like them more than they liked me. I realize now that the reason for that was that sissies and girls had a lot in common.

Sissies always had a different type Christmas from the rest of us. They got a lot of socks and, of course, dozens of handkerchiefs. They also, without exception, got chemistry sets for Christmas.

My sissy friend Brooks (his mother called him Brooksie) was always careful to protect and take care of his toys (another mark of a sissy). Every single Christmas, Brooks got a brand-new chemistry set and was real careful with it. So by the time he was about thirteen, he had a basement full of chemistry sets. He called it his laboratory and nobody else was allowed to come in. Nobody, that is, until one particular Sunday when the entire East Point Fire Department got to see his laboratory. They were invited in when Brooks mixed the wrong stuff together and blew one wall slap out of his basement.

Brooks was blistered pretty bad in the explosion and had to come to school wearing bandages on his face and hands. We were all pretty moved by his condition, except for the class clown and sissy-hater extreme, Poot Monroe.

Poot said, "Hey, teacher, how come old Brooks is comin' to school lookin' like a mummy?"

Miss Neese said, "We mustn't make fun of Brooks. He is the victim of a horrible accident."

"Yeah," Poot said, "but he sure does look like a mummy."

The damage was done. From that day on, everyone called Brooks, "Mummy." It was a milestone day in the history of sissydom, however, because on that day Brooks became the first sissy ever to have a nickname.

6

A Dreaded Visit
From Western Union

I WAS ABOUT six years old when World War II started, and while it began suddenly and dramatically for the rest of the world, in my mind it started gradually. I guess my tender years made it difficult to comprehend what was happening.

My first memory, for some strange reason, was the music:

"Let's remember Pearl Harbor as we go to meet
   the foe,
Let's remember Pearl Harbor as we did the
   Alamo."

"We will always remember how they died for
   liberty,
Let's remember Pearl Harbor and go on to
   victory."

Ludlow Porch

There were more songs, like:

"Praise the Lord and pass the ammunition.
Praise the Lord we're not going fishin'.

"Praise the Lord and pass the ammunition,
And we'll all stay free.

"Yes, the sky pilot said, you got to give him credit,
'Cause a son of a gun of a gunner was he."

I heard them on the radio and even around town.

As I learned to read, I began to make out the little signs in store windows that said, "Remember Pearl Harbor." Soon I was able to put the songs and the window stickers together.

Finally I realized what was going on. The Japs had bombed us, and now we were fighting them and the Germans as well.

I never worried much about the outcome of the war, because it was only logical that we would win. Everybody said that God was on our side. It just made sense.

I did worry, however, about my uncles going off to war. They had always been around home, and I didn't like the idea of their suddenly being away. Nonetheless, I was proud to know that my folks were fighting, and I was bad to brag about my uncles to the other boys. I knew that the war couldn't last long with my folks doing the fighting.

The war brought many changes to our lives. One of the most obvious was that all of the young men were gone. There was even a song about that:

"They're either too young or too old,
They're either too bold or too grassy green.

"What's good is in the Army,
What's left will never harm me."

New signs went up in the post office. They showed a picture of a Japanese soldier with his hand cupped behind his ear. The caption read, "The Japs Are Listening." Another poster warned, "Loose Lips Sink Ships," and yet another said, "Slap a Jap. Buy War Bonds."

It's funny how any time I think about World War II, the memories come rushing back.

I remember the blackouts when my mother and I would sit in our room listening to the air raid siren and watching the lights go off all over our neighborhood. It was fun, but it was scary.

I remember our Victory Garden. Our hearts were in the right place, but if we had had to depend on it for food, we would have been in deep trouble.

I remember the radio blaring forth with, "Lucky Strike's Green has gone to war."

I remember shoe rationing. You could only have two pair a year, and for a little boy who was rough on his shoes, it was tough. I spent many hours in Moody's Shoe Shop waiting to get replacement soles and heels.

I remember meatless Tuesday and what a shock it was to not be able to get anything but lettuce and tomato sandwiches at the B & F Grill on Tuesday.

I remember gasoline rationing and how folks were walking or riding bicycles for the first time. When the rationing tickets were gone, you couldn't buy gas, period. You soon learned that joy riding was out of the question.

It seemed to me that everybody I knew was involved in the war effort in some way, and I wanted to do my share by growing up and joining the service. The combination of seeing uniforms and the war movies was all I needed to make me ready to haul my seven-year-old self off to war. It was perfectly clear to me that John Wayne and William Bendix were having more fun than I was.

Instead, I had to content myself by buying stamps and sticking them in my book until I had enough to turn them into a war bond. I also cut both ends out of tin cans, stomped them flat and took little bundles of them to school.

We even saved our bacon grease, although I never did figure out why. I saved newspapers, tinfoil and scrap iron.

I also believed the signs in the post office about loose lips sinking ships; therefore, I made it a point never to discuss troop movements with anyone.

In the midst of efforts to help win the war, I suddenly realized that some things were missing from my young life. For one thing, Double Bubble gum was gone. As a matter of fact, all gum was gone. Juicy Fruit had always been available in my mother's pocket, but that damn Hitler had taken care of that.

The pennies went from the lovely copper I had always known to a tinny look that I didn't trust. Had the Japanese stolen our copper?

Margarine was no longer yellow, it was white. But at least they gave us a little packet of coloring to squish up and make it turn yellow.

We couldn't buy Coca-Cola. We couldn't buy pork and beans and, in the name of God, we couldn't even buy a Hershey bar. War was hell for a seven-year-old.

We had air raid drills at school, and everyone knew exactly what to do if the Germans ever bombed us. Mr. Allen was our neighborhood Air Raid Warden. I thought how lucky he was to be the only person allowed on the street during an air raid warning.

New words crept into my vocabulary. Words like: *Bataan, Corrigador, 4-F, incendiary bomb, black market, Mussolini, draft dodger, Jeep, Gold Star Mother, invasion, tiger tank, commando, recap, Rosie the Riveter, buck private, Colin Kelly, Eisenhower, Patton and Tojo, B-24, P-38 and Messerschmidt.*

Then the war was all I knew. I heard on the radio that Joe Louis was in the Army. I read in the funnies that Joe Palooka was also in the Army.

Ludlow Porch

The Andrews Sisters were singing about the Boogie-Woogie Bugle Boy of Company B.

Roy Acuff assured the world that there would be "smoke on the water, smoke on the sea, / When our Army and Navy overtake the enemy."

President Roosevelt said there was nothing to be afraid of.

My friend Pig said his brother Ed was going to kick the shit out of the Japs as soon as he got out of boot camp.

My Uncle Simpson sent me a sailor hat from the Pacific. It was my proudest possession.

My Uncle Walt sent me his old Corporal stripes. I got my mother to sew them on my winter coat.

I was playing in the front yard when the Western Union boy peddled up on his bicycle. Even at my young age, I knew what that meant. I remember thinking, My grandmother is here alone, and Western Union is coming to tell her that one of her sons has been killed by the Japs or Germans. I don't think she'll be able to stand it. I wish there was a grown-up here. What will I do? Oh, God, please! Let the Western Union boy go away and come back when there's a grown-up here. What will I say to her? What can I do?

He got off his bike and walked up the front steps. I raced down the hallway and met him at the front door. I was going to hide the telegram and not give it up till there was a grown-up there to be with my grandmother.

"I'll take it," I said.

"Are you old enough to sign for it?" he asked.

I was in the process of lying about my age when my grandmother appeared beside me at the front door.

"What is it, sonny boy?"

"A telegram, ma'am."

She signed for it. Then with tears running down her beautiful wrinkled face, she said, "I'll sit right down on the sofa and you read it to me."

"Let's read it later," I said, still stalling for adult company.

"No," she said. "We must be brave. You read it to me now."

I could tell she was crying, even though she wasn't making any noise. Tears were cascading down her cheeks.

I started to read the telegram. "It is with deep regret . . ."

My grandmother started to cry out. She was sobbing and saying, "My baby. My baby's dead."

She was on her feet wringing her hands and walking from room to room, sobbing louder and louder. I followed her and tried to finish reading the telegram at the same time. "He's not dead, Mama. He's not dead. He's only wounded. Listen, Mama. The telegram says he's only wounded."

"Which one?" she sobbed.

"Tommy. It's Tommy, Mama. Tommy's tough. The German's couldn't hurt Tom. You'll see. He'll be fine."

He was fine. He came home years later, tall and proud and healthy and handsome. He was my hero then, and now forty years later, he's still my hero.

About that time I heard a man named MacArthur say on a MovieTone newsreel, "I shall return." I was impressed by how much he sounded like God Almighty.

Then more new words forced their way into my vocabulary. Strange new words like "Iwo Jima" and "Saipan." We heard that my Uncle Buddy Hanson and the rest of the Marine Corps were jumping from island to island, killing Japs till hell wouldn't have it. My Uncle Buddy would teach the Japs to mess around with Old Glory.

From the other side of the world, the word came suddenly. The war in Europe was over. The Germans had finally given up. Hitler was dead, and the war in Europe was over.

The beginning of the end had started. All we had to do was send the troops from Europe to join our boys in the Pacific, and we could knock the Japs' hat in the creek.

There were many rumors about the surrender of the Japanese, but they all proved false. The war in the Pacific dragged on.

Then three more words burst into our language, never to leave again: "Atomic," "Hiroshima," and "Nagasaki."

It was over. They called it V-J Day.

The celebration in Atlanta was wild. The streets

were full of people. They kissed. They hugged. They danced and drank whiskey straight out of the bottle. Bands played and fireworks went off. And at 322 Spring Avenue, East Point, Georgia, a lady with auburn hair streaked with gray spent the evening on her knees. Her babies were coming home and she was celebrating the only way she knew how. She was thanking her God.

7

Winning the War
But Losing the Battle

WHEN THE WAR was finally over, the service men all started to come home. It was a wonderful thing to see. Those who had left as boys now were returning home as men.

They had spent four years growing up the hard way. Many of them had lost their Southern accents and their innocence. They had been all over the world and had seen death many times over. They had walked the streets of Rome, Paris and Tokyo.

But finally they were home and wanted to make up for the time they had lost. They were looking for ways to take their first bites from the American pie.

Many of them had saved a lot of cash. After all, where they had been, there was nothing to spend it on. Suddenly, new businesses started springing up everywhere. There was the Veterans' gas station, the Veterans' tire store, and our next-door neighbor was involved in some way with the Veterans' cab company.

We were glad for him. He had been a little wild before the war, so we were all delighted that he had settled down enough to get involved in his own business. He also bought a second-hand car (new cars were about impossible to find), which would have been further evidence of his maturity except for one thing: He had twin smitties mounted on the car. They were so loud that you could hear him coming two blocks away. And unfortunately for all of us, he went to work every morning about five A.M.

It was the practice at that time to warm up your car for about fifteen minutes before driving off, and our neighbor liked to gun his engine while it warmed up. With those twin smitties in place, it sounded like he had brought the war in Europe home with him.

When he was sure that everyone in the state of Georgia was awake, he would put his car in low gear, pop the clutch, and the tires would scream like all the banshees in hell were trying to get out. He would burn rubber for about half a block.

There was no way for anybody to sleep through his morning departure. It was the talk of the neighborhood, but nobody would say anything to him. After all, he was a veteran, and all the grown-ups said, "He just needs a little time to find himself. Sooner or later he'll realize that he's disturbing the whole neighborhood, and he'll be all right. Yes, sir, he's OK, just a little high-strung. He'll be OK. You'll see. He'll be just fine."

My Uncle Harry (who was just a few years older than me) and I had the problem scoped out much better than the grown-ups. We remembered this fellow had been an ass before the war, and apparently he remained the same. He really didn't care if he disturbed the neighborhood or not. He was arrogant and worthless, and if this problem was going to be solved, we figured it was up to us to do so.

We gave some thought to killing him and getting a good night's sleep, but even at our young ages, we knew that would screw up our whole summer if we got caught.

We decided on an equally violent but less permanent solution to the situation.

One night, we stayed awake until after midnight when we knew for sure that everyone else was asleep. We slipped quietly out of the house — just me, Harry, fifty feet of rope and a Boy Scout knife.

This fellow's car was parked on the street in front of his house. First we tied the rope to the back bumper; then, crawling on our bellies like two delinquent commandos, we ran the rope from the bumper, across the sidewalk, through a hedge and across the lawn.

Next came the dangerous part. We were outside his screened-in porch lying on our bellies. We took out the Boy Scout knife and cut a small hole in the screen near the floor. We fed the end of the rope through the hole onto the porch.

Slowly and silently, we opened the door and I

crawled onto the porch. It seemed like it took an hour. Harry fed the end of the rope to me, and I tied it securely around the leg of a giant green rocking chair. Then I crawled back out onto the lawn and we sneaked home.

We had done it. Now all we had to do was stay awake and watch the fun. The hours crept by, but finally we heard it: *Vroooom, Vroooom.*

He warmed the car up for what seemed like an eternity. Meanwhile, we were peeping out of the window and counting the seconds. Two little boys watching and waiting for their plan to reach its violent conclusion.

Then it happened. He dropped the car into low and popped the clutch. The tires screamed, the slack popped out of the rope and that great big old rocking chair was airborne, surrounded by the screen from the porch. It cleared the hedge and hit the ground the first time in the middle of the street.

By the time our veteran friend realized that he was being followed by a rocking chair and a screened-in porch, it was too late. The noise had been terrible, and suddenly every light in the neighborhood was on to witness his embarrassment.

Harry and I didn't turn on our light. As a matter of fact, we were soon fast asleep with smiles on our faces.

Our caper was the talk of the neighborhood for days, but we never told a soul . . . until now.

8

Radio was an Earful
In the Old Days

WHEN FOUL WEATHER or dark of night forced us inside, we turned to the greatest entertainment source of our generation — the radio.

My earliest memories of radio are when I was about four or five years old. I was alone at home every day with my grandmother, and the radio was almost always tuned to a soap opera. I became familiar with the names and the theme songs — *Oxydol's Own Ma Perkins; Lorenzo Jones; One Man's Family; Mary Noble, Backstage Wife;* and *Stella Dallas.*

There were other daytime shows that I enjoyed more than the soaps. For some strange reason, I always liked "Queen For a Day" with Jack Bailey. I never understood how human misery could be so entertaining, but it was. I also never understood how a widow woman whose children were starving and living in an unheated shack could be so excited about winning a week's vacation in Hawaii and three rooms of carpet from the Looms of Mohawk.

There was also a rather strange show that came out of Chicago called, "Welcome Traveler," hosted by a very nice man named Tommy Bartlett. He had a studio audience and just talked to them and gave them gifts. I suspect that's the only reason they showed up.

The thing I remember most about early-morning radio was the jingles. They made products familiar with jingles that became familiar to generations of Americans:

"Super Suds, Super Suds,
  Lots more suds from Super Suds,
  Richer, longer lasting, too,
  They're the suds with super-doo-oo-oo."

"Rinso White, Rinso Blue,
  Happy little wash day song."

"Tide's in, dirt's out,
  Tide's in, dirt's out,
  Tide gets clothes cleaner than any soap,
  T-I-D-E, Tide."

"Duz does everything."

Radio commercials also taught us how to be beautiful and smell nice:

"Dream girl, dream girl,

Beautiful, Luster Creme girl,
You owe your crowning glory to a
Luster Creme shampoo."

"Halo, everybody, Halo,
Halo is the shampoo that glorifies your hair.
Halo, everybody, halo,
So Halo shampoo, halo."

"Lifebuoy really stops BEEEEEE-
OHHHHHHHH."

"Ivory soap. Ninety-nine and forty-four one
hundredths percent pure. It floats."

"L-A-V-A, L-A-V-A."

We were also told exactly what to eat and drink:

"Whiiizzz! The best nickel candy there
izzzzzz."
"You can say that again."
"All right, I will: Whiiizzz, best nickel
candy there is!"

"B.R.O.C.K. Buy a Brock today."

"Pepsi-Cola hits the spot,
Twelve full ounces, that's a lot,
Twice as much for a nickel, too,
Pepsi-Cola is the drink for you.

Nickel, nickel, nickel, nickel,
Trickle, trickle, trickle, trickle."

"Royal pudding,
Rich, rich, rich with flavor,
Smooth, smooth as silk,
More food energy than sweet fresh milk."

If you didn't feel well, radio had all the answers:

"Anacin is like a doctor's prescription . . . that is not one but a combination of medically proven active ingredients. Perhaps your doctor or dentist has given you a few Anacin tables to relieve headaches, neuritis or neuralgia. That's Anacin, A-N-A-C-I-N. Anacin."

About 3:30 in the afternoon, the children's shows started to come on. No matter what I was doing, I always ran home to hear them. There were not a lot of programs on for young folks, but what we had were wonderful and we listened to them every single day. We couldn't miss an episode because all the programs were "cliffhangers." We had to listen every day to follow the plots.

I would sit and stare at the radio and wait for the announcer to shout, "Look! Up in the sky! It's a bird! It's a plane! It's Superman!" Then I would sit spellbound for the entire fifteen minute show, until the announcer closed by saying, "Tune in tomorrow for the further adventures of Suuuperman!"

I was what Tom Mix called a "straight shooter." Tom told us day after day that "straight shooters always win." I sent off for every premium ever offered on his show. It was easy; all you had to do was send fifteen cents along with a box top to the Ralston Purina Company, Checkerboard Square, St. Louis, Missouri.

I was also a member of Captain Midnight's "Secret Squadron." And like every other boy in America, I was a fan of "Jack Armstrong, All-American Boy." Jack was sponsored by Wheaties, and all boys worth their salt knew every word of his theme song:

> "Wave the flag for Hudson High, boys,
> Show them how we stand!
> Ever shall our team be champion
> Known throughout the land.
> Rah, Rah, Boola, Boola, Boola!

> "Have you tried Wheaties?
> They're whole wheat with all of the bran.
> Won't you try Wheaties?
> For wheat is the best food of man.

> "They're crispy and crunchy the whole year through,
> Jack Armstrong never tires of them and neither will you.
> So just buy Wheaties, the best breakfast food in the land."

Another of my favorites was "Hop Harrigan, America's Ace of the Airwaves, with his best friend, Tank Tinker." The show always started with the sound of an airplane, and then you could hear Hop's voice over the sound of the plane.

"CX-4 calling control tower. CX-4 calling control tower. Standing by! OK, this is Hop Harrigan . . . coming in!"

"The Green Hornet" was one of my all-time favorites. I would sit staring at the radio as the "Flight of the Bumblebee" came on and the announcer said in a deep rich voice, "The Green Hornet . . . He hunts the biggest of all game — public enemies who try to destroy America . . . with his faithful valet, Britt Reid, daring young publisher, matches wits with the underworld, risking his life that criminals and racketeers within the law may feel its weight by the sting of the Green Hornet!"

And who could ever forget "The Masked Rider of the Plains"? Almost every child I knew was a member of the Lone Ranger Safety Club, even though we had a little trouble with the title. We called him the *Long* Ranger.

Children all over America would sit by their radios, eager to hear the first notes of the "William Tell Overture." Then the announcer, in his big booming voice, would say, "A fiery horse with the speed of light, a cloud of dust and a hearty 'Hi-yo, Silver.' The Lone Ranger!" The music would get louder and then real soft as the announcer continued, "With his faithful Indian companion, Tonto, the daring and resourceful masked rider of the plains led the fight for law and order in the early western United States. Nowhere in the pages of history can one find a greater champion of justice. Return with us now to those thrilling days of yesteryear. (This is where you could hear the hoofbeats.) From out of the past comes the thundering hoofbeats of the great horse, Silver. The Lone Ranger rides again!"

Then you could hear the Ranger: "Come on, Silver. Let's go, big fellow. Hi-yo, Silver, away."

The show always closed with a message for all the boys and girls in the Lone Ranger Safety Club: drink our milk, be careful crossing the street and always mind our moms.

As good as the daytime radio was, prime time was better. It was something to behold. The whole family would gather in the parlor after supper and get ready for whatever was about to come.

Can anybody ever forget Wednesday night with "Mr. District Attorney," brought to us by Bristol-Myers, makers of Ipana for the smile of beauty and Sal Hepatica for the smile of health? Those folks knew what they were doing. They covered a toothpaste and a laxative in one short commercial sentence. Then the announcer would say, "Mr. District Attorney . . . champion of the people . . . defender of truth . . . guardian of our fundamental rights to life, liberty and the pursuit of happiness."

Mr. District Attorney would come in and say, "And it shall be my duty as district attorney not only to prosecute to the limit of the law all persons accused of crimes perpetrated within the county, but to defend with equal vigor the rights and privileges of all its citizens."

On Tuesday nights at 9:30 our dial was always set on NBC. We were ready to spend the evening at 79 Wistful Vista with "Fibber McGee and Molly." It was a fun and relaxing half hour when you got to visit with a lot of old friends — Harlow Wilcox, Doc Gamble, Throck Morton, P. Gildersleeve, Mayor La Trivia, Wallace Wimple, Beulah the Maid and, of course, Little Sis.

It kept us smiling for thirty minutes and sold millions of cans of Johnson Wax.

There were so many more. How could we have survived the war years without the mirth and madness of our beloved Red Skelton, and his cast of characters? Junior, the mean little kid; Clem Kadiddlehopper; Deadeye; Willy Lump-Lump; J. Newton Numbskull; Bolivar Shagnasty and lots more. In my opinion, Red Skelton was much better on radio and in the movies than he ever was on TV.

And let's not forget "Lum and Abner," those two wonderful guys from the Jot 'Em Down Store in Pine Ridge, Arkansas.

Precious memories, how they linger:

> Little Orphan Annie, Yours Truly Johnny
> Dollar, Your Hit Parade, Young Widder

Brown, Duffy's Tavern, Blondie, Big Town, Beulah, The Adventures of Ozzie and Harriet, People Are Funny, The Quiz Kids, Big John and Spanky, Amos 'n' Andy, The Bing Crosby Show, Jack Benny, The Breakfast Club, The Cisco Kid, Death Valley Days, Dr. Christian, Dr. I.Q., Father Knows Best, The Kate Smith Show, Al Jolson's Kraft Music Hall, Bobby Benson and the B-Bar B. Riders, Hopalong Cassidy, The First Nighter, Dragnet, I Love A Mystery, Suspense and The Inner Sanctum.

Oh, how I loved radio, the theater of the mind. Say what you will about TV, but it has never reached the inner mind or imagination like radio.

It's been gone for more than thirty years now. But still on Tuesday nights at 9:30 I occasionally turn the radio on, hoping just one more time to take that short trip back to see Fibber McGee and Molly at 79 Wistful Vista.

9

We Found Friends, Family in the Funnies

YEARS BEFORE I knew that newspapers had front pages or sports pages, I was a big fan of the funnies. They're called comic strips now, but to me they will forevermore be the funnies.

There was "Henry," a little bald-headed boy that I always imagined to be about my age. Henry was not only funny, but he managed to be funny without talking.

One of the things I admired most about Henry was his freedom. His parents obviously were not very strict, because he went where he wanted to and did pretty much what he wanted. And I don't think I ever saw him in school. Nonetheless, he never got into any serious trouble and I always identified with old Henry.

"The Little King" was another of my favorites. We never knew his name or the kingdom over which he ruled, but he did some unkingly things, and that made us laugh.

"Lil Abner" and all his family and friends in Dogpatch had the whole country laughing. The adventures of Abner, Daisy Mae and Mammy and Pappy Yokum was something we anticipated every day. Earthquake McGoon, Lonesome Polecat and Hairless Joe became our friends. Big Barnsmell was the inside man at the skunk works, and Senator Jack S. Phogbound represented Dogpatch in the U.S. Senate. We couldn't wait for November to come around to see how Lil Abner got away from Daisy Mae on Sadie Hawkins Day. And do you remember Kickapoo Joy Juice?

I have fond memories of sitting on my grandfather's lap while he read "Captain and the Kids" to me. Hans and Fritz, the twin little boys who were the main characters, became so real to me that I felt like I knew them on a first-name basis. I also knew the grumpy Captain, the Inspector, Mama and the archenemy of the twins, the sissy Rollo.

"The Gumps" were a national favorite, but they were a little mature for my young taste. I classified them with my grandmother's beloved radio soap operas. I remember the grown-ups laughing and talking about Andy Gump, his wife, Min, and their young son, Chester.

The Gumps looked strange to me because they had no chins. I remember thinking to myself, How can they put on a pillow case without a chin?

I guess all little boys loved airplanes, and I was no exception. "Smilin' Jack" was about airplanes and was therefore immensely popular. Smilin' Jack was a handsome son of a gun with a little Clark Gable mustache. He was married to Joy and had a son named Jungle Jolly. His best friends were Downwind Jackson and Fat Stuff, who always popped buttons off his shirt only to have them caught in mid-air by a featherless little chicken.

"Smokey Stover" was a fireman who was funnier than the law allowed. The fire chief was Chief Cash U. Nutt. In the thirties and forties, America had a love affair going with old Smokey Stover.

"Blondie and Dagwood" also swept the country. In the beginning there was just Blondie and Dagwood, but soon Baby Dumpling came along, followed by his little sister, Cookie, and their fuzzy-faced dog, Daisy. This comic strip was so loved that it spawned a highly successful radio show and a series of movies starring Penny Singleton and Arthur Lake as the title characters.

We all laughed as Dagwood ran for the bus every morning and invariably ran over Mr. Beasley, the poor mailman. It was enough to make a dog laugh. And don't forget Herb Woodley, Dagwood's obnoxious next-door neighbor or Mr. Dithers, the boss.

The real name of another popular strip was "Bringing Up Father," but we all called it Maggie and Jiggs. It was the story of a brick mason (Jiggs) and his wife, Maggie, a washerwoman. They were very poor until one day they won the Irish Sweepstakes and became instant millionaires.

Maggie turned at once into a rich snob who

wanted to forget her roots. Jiggs, on the other hand, just wanted to slip away from Maggie and meet his old chums at Dinty Moore's Tavern for some corned beef and cabbage and a few hands of pinochle. We all loved and felt a little sorry for poor old Jiggs.

I think the reason we liked Maggie and Jiggs so much was because we were poor and enjoyed reading about one of our kind who suddenly came into money and could have whatever he wanted. While we laughed at Jiggs for trying to slip out of their penthouse to get away from Maggie, we also admired the fact that money had not changed him.

But I always knew that if old Jiggs could ever sit down at my grandmother's table and try her milk gravy and biscuits, he would soon forget about corned beef and cabbage.

"Dick Tracy" was every little boy's favorite detective. The stories were good, and Tracy never let us down in his pursuit of the lawless, like Prune Face and Flat Top. With his partner, Pat Patton, he taught us that there was only one way to handle a crook — shoot him in the head.

I used to worry a lot about Dick's family. He had a delightful wife and a lovely child that he never went home to see. He would work all the time, sometimes not going home for a year or two. I guess if it worked out for Dick and Tess, then it was nobody else's business.

"Mandrake the Magician" entertained me as he gestured hypnotically. Princess Narda was beautiful, and his African sidekick, Lothor, made the bad guys run for cover.

"Little Orphan Annie" and her dog, Sandy, bored me in their endless search for Daddy Warbucks. But I read about them anyway.

I loved "Alley Oop." He was a caveman who could get into a time machine and go anywhere he pleased. One week you'd find him fighting at the side of King Arthur. The next week he would be in a blue or gray uniform, fighting for his life at Gettysburg.

In a fight of any kind, Alley Oop was almost invincible. When he started to swing that stone ax, his enemies would be scattered in all directions.

He lived in the Kingdom of Moo and rode a dinosaur named Dinny. His friend was the King of the Kingdom of Moo, King Guzzle. The inventor of the time machine was Professor Wonmug. His demented assistant was named Oscar Boom.

Alley Oop's girlfriend was Oola, and she was a good-looking old girl. Alley Oop spent a lot of time bashing in the head of folks who had done Oola wrong in one way or another. I was royally entertained.

"Ozark Ike" was a great big handsome baseball and football player. He played for a major league team called the Bugs. Ozark Ike quickly became the hero of little boys everywhere, and we watched the funnies every day to see when he would hit his next homer or run for his next touchdown.

"Joe Palooka" was one of my favorites. Joe was

81

the heavyweight boxing champ, and to me he was everything a great champion should be. He was quite unassuming, never bragged and never said anything bad about his opponents or anybody else.

He was a true friend to his pal and manager, Knobby Walsh, a good husband to his wife, Ann Howe Palooka, and father to their adopted son, Max.

When World War II came along, Joe Palooka was one of the first comic strip characters to go into service. He joined the Army as a private.

I think Joe Palooka was one of my first idols. I learned a lot about fair play and sportsmanship from him. I wish some of our present-day boxers could spend a little time with Joe Palooka.

"The Phantom" was another strip that most little boys watched for. He wore a mask, a purple body suit and two .45 automatics. He had a gray wolf named Devil and lived in a cave shaped like a huge skull. The thing that most caught my imagination as a child was his ring. It was shaped like a skull, and when the Phantom hit a bad guy in the jaw, it left a skull mark on his jaw forever. Boy, oh boy, wouldn't it be something to have your very own skull ring? Nobody would be fool enough to mess with a ten-year-old who could leave a skull mark on their jaw forever.

The Phantom hung around with a Pygmy named Guran. I couldn't identify with that since I had never seen a real Pygmy, and the only thing I knew about them was that Tarzan didn't like them much.

But the ones that the Phantom bossed around seemed to be pleasant enough for their size.

The Phantom rode a great white horse named Hero and had a girlfriend named Diana Palmer. I could never figure out what he saw in her. She was always getting into trouble with bad guys from pirates to Nazis to out-and-out white trash crooks. I knew deep down that if the Phantom didn't have to keep rescuing her, he could spend all his time having fun in the jungle. No matter what dumb things she did, however, it was apparent to me that he loved her better than a hog loves slop. When he finally married Diana, I lost interest in the Phantom. I just knew that she was going to nag him about hitting folks in the jaw with his skull ring.

"Red Ryder" was a wonderful cowboy comic strip hero. He lived on a ranch near the little town of Rimrock, Colorado. He managed the ranch with the help of his grumpy but lovable aunt, whom everybody called simply, "The Dutchess."

Red hung around the ranch until old Sheriff Newt would call on him for help. Then he would put on his battered old hat, saddle his black horse, Thunder, and head out to get after some bad guys.

His adventures were always shared by a little Navajo orphan that he had adopted. His name was Little Beaver, and every child I knew secretly wished that he could be Little Beaver and ride out of Rimrock with Red Ryder in search of adventure. We flocked to the Red Ryder movies and listened faithfully to his talks on the radio. We even had

Daisy Red Ryder BB guns.

"Secret Agent X-9" was another of my favorites. During the Second World War, he caught Nazi spies till the cows came home. I liked him because he never arrested the bad guys. He either knocked them off cliffs, blew 'em up, shot 'em or set 'em on fire. I didn't know a whole lot about Japanese or German spies, but I knew that jail was too good for the sorry no-accounts.

"Buzz Sawyer" helped in the war effort, as did Terry, of "Terry and the Pirates," and "Steve Canyon."

"Captain Easy" and Wash Tubbs also helped to fight the Japanese.

For the science fiction fans, "Buck Rogers" was great and "Flash Gordon" was even better.

I loved and respected "Mark Trail," who was teaching about wildlife conservation thirty years before the rest of the world wised up. I like his sweetheart, Cherry, and his beautiful dog, Andy.

My childhood was filled with adventure and action, thanks to my funny paper friends. Wouldn't it be a red letter day if we could renew our childhood love affair with the funnies again?

To fly the wing with Terry Lee.

To sit and laugh on the front porch of "Our Boarding House" with my old friend, Major Hoople.

To swing through the jungle with my adventurous sidekick, Tarzan.

To swing a broadsword in battle beside Prince Valiant.

To ride to work on a streetcar, sitting beside Tillie the Toiler.

To watch Toots and Casper survive during the middle of the Depression.

To go for an ice cream with Nancy and Sluggo.

To share the worldwide adventures of Captain Easy and his little friend, Wash Tubbs.

To fly off the deck of an aircraft carrier with Buzz Sawyer at the controls.

And wouldn't it be something if just once before I die, I could walk one more log with the world's favorite hillbilly, Snuffy Smith? Barney Google in his top hat always knocked me out.

It's hard to explain, but in the carefree, eternally warm days of my youth, the folks in the funnies were my friends. They made me laugh and cry, and they taught me valuable lessons. I enjoyed their company, and now I miss them a lot.

10

The Price of Admission? A Zillion Circulars

THE FAIRFAX WAS the only movie in my hometown. It was old and dirty, but to me it was a wonderland of fun.

I learned early on that all things were possible there. Roy Rogers could beat up five evil men and never lose his hat at the Fairfax. Charlie Chan was never wrong and always knew who the murderer was. Tarzan could kill an alligator with nothing but his knife at the Fairfax. Moe could drag a saw across Curly's head and never even hurt him.

It was, indeed, a wonderful, wonderful place.

Once the movie started, you forgot about the popcorn machine that had not been cleaned in your lifetime, about the yellow grease that clung to it like grass to a meadow.

You forgot about the men's room that smelled like the urine of the ages had been collected there.

It never occurred to you that a balcony for blacks

was wrong, or that the wooden seats were uncomfortable. You forgot that your feet literally stuck to the floor because it was so dirty. You never stopped to wonder why the Fairfax was nicknamed "The Bug House."

We gathered there every Saturday to find out what happened in the serials. For nine cents, we were treated to a half day of unequalled entertainment. The show usually began with a B-western that consisted of four fist fights, two horse chases and at least two gun battles.

The heroes were always the same — Roy Rogers, Gene Autry, Tim Holt, Lash LaRue, Charles Starrett, Bob Steele, Whip Wilson, Eddie Dean, Johnny Mack Brown or Jimmy Wakely. Most of them had sidekicks, such as Gabby Hayes, Smiley Burnette, Chico Rafferty, Raymond Hatton, and, of course, Al St. John as Fuzzy Q. Jones.

The second feature was usually either Charlie Chan, The East Side Kids, The Falcon, The Saint or a cheapo version of Robin Hood, Boston Blackie or Zorro.

But the two B-pictures were only the beginning of our Saturday entertainment. There was also Pathe or MovieTone news, a cartoon and a short comedy, either the Three Stooges, Leon Erroll or Arthur Kennedy.

The only thing that ever stood between us and all this fun was the nine cents admission. I know that doesn't sound like a lot of money today, but I missed many a Saturday of fun because I couldn't come up with it.

There were several ways around this problem, however. For openers, you could attempt to "slip in." But this plan had at least two drawbacks for me: First, my mother would have been so embarrassed if I had been caught that she would have been unable to show her face in public; second, she would have turned me into a carrot. That's why I seldom tried to slip in.

Two other ways were safer but a lot more work. In those days, there was a flour company named Capitola. In the bottom of every bag of flour, they put metal tokens about the size of a half dollar. These were called Capitola tokens, and you would get into the movie free with a token. It was always easy to spot the kids in line at the movie who had Capitola tokens: They were the ones with flour all the way to their elbows.

There was one other way to get into the movie without giving up your hard-earned nine cents. The Fairfax gave out circulars from time to time, telling about their coming attractions. If you would distribute about a zillion circulars, they would give you two free passes to the theater.

It was a big job to give out a zillion circulars, but it was worth it. After all, it only took all day and the passes were worth a grand total of eighteen cents. Where else could you make that kind of money?

The first time I got involved in the venture, I put circulars behind windshield wipers and screen doors until I thought I was going to drop, but the reward was great: two free passes. The next time I went to pick up circulars, my friend and idol, Pig, went along. We each were handed our zillion circulars.

"Where are you going to give out your circulars?" I asked Pig.

He looked both ways to make sure no one was listening. Then he said, "I'm going down behind the pump house."

"Why are you going there? Nobody lives down there," I said.

"I know, but there's a sewer down there."

"What are you going to do there?" I asked again.

He said he was going to "ditch" his circulars.

"What does that mean?"

"Come on," he said, "I'll show you."

When we got there, he threw all his circulars in the sewer. It seemed like a good idea, so I threw mine in the sewer, too.

"What do we do now?" I asked.

"We wait a while, then we go back to the Fairfax and get our passes."

We waited around for two or three hours and then went back and got our passes.

I would like to report that my conscience started to hurt me and I immediately mended my evil ten-year-old ways. The fact of the matter is, however, that I thought it was a wonderful scam. All I had to do was pick up the circulars, throw them down the sewer, and get my theater passes.

It was about twenty-five years before I had even a small twinge of conscience. By then the Fairfax had closed and the circulars were too wet to be of any use to anyone, so I didn't worry about it anymore.

The Fairfax was not only the scene of many on-screen adventures, it was also the scene of many off-screen misadventures.

After a couple of weeks of the same serials, my friend Raymond got the idea that the shows were not as exciting as they could be. So he spent one Friday night catching lightnin' bugs and putting them in a mayonnaise jar.

The next morning he smuggled the jar into the Fairfax.

The movie was extra crowded that day, and somewhere between a Bob Steele western and *The March of Time*, Raymond took the top off of his mayonnaise jar and, unnoticed, sat it under the seat beside him. In about ten minutes, the theater was filled with hundreds of lightnin' bugs.

The ushers were helpless, and we were laughing and applauding like crazy. We were not applauding because of the lightnin' bugs, but because when they had made their presence known, our black friends in the balcony had started to sing, "Glow Worm," at the top of their lungs.

Through the whole thing, Raymond looked neither to his left nor his right. He just sat there staring at the screen and shoving popcorn into his mouth. The management never suspected good old Raymond of being in charge of the lightnin' bug caper. That's when I learned that quiet kids bear close watching.

Two more theaters eventually were built in East Point, and Lord knows I spent many hours in them. They were cleaner and closer to my house, but somehow they never had the appeal to me that "The Bug House" did.

I've often thought if that old picture show could talk, it would tell many stories about those wild matinees. How many young folks did it see get their first kiss?

It was sure not much of a movie by today's standards, but it was a gathering place for memories, and the older I get, the more important that becomes.

11

Making Money and Time
At Glover's Pharmacy

I DON'T THINK my boyhood crowd was any more industrious than today's youngsters, but I do believe the times made us more aware of money. There was literally no money around to be shared with us by our parents, so if we were going to have any spending loot, it was up to us to make it.

One of my first ventures was selling figs, which grew abundantly on bushes in our yard. I would pick the figs and sell them door-to-door for ten cents a quart. If I worked hard, I could make about two dollars a week. That was big money to me, and I probably would have done it year 'round and grown rich. But, of course, the figs wouldn't cooperate.

I collected and sold soft drink bottles at two cents a piece, but that required a lot of bending over. I tried cutting grass for awhile, but that was highly competitive and also seasonal. I was looking for steady income.

One summer my Uncle Harry and two of his friends got an *Atlanta Constitution* paper route and needed somebody to help them. I fell heir to a new job.

The job was fun and paid pretty well. I particularly liked being with the big boys, and being out on the streets before daylight was an exciting and wonderful thing. And best of all, breakfast was also furnished.

Let me explain. It wasn't a real breakfast, like bacon and eggs; it was a special breakfast. We knew that on Mondays, for example, the Dutch Oven bakery left doughnuts at Mrs. Brown's house, so we helped ourselves. Also on Mondays, the milkman left chocolate milk at another door and orangeade at yet another. We simply walked around the neighborhood checking front porches. We would then sit under the street light at Spring and Maple Streets and breakfast like European royalty. Then we would throw our paper and bottles down the sewer and deliver our papers.

I'll never understand how we did that every morning and never got caught.

I assume the poor neighbors thought they were being shorted by the delivery man, when all the while four young hellions were eating like kings. We were growing fat and the delivery guys were catching hell.

I can only hope for two things: (1) that none of them got into too much trouble because of our actions, and (2) that the statute of limitations has run out on the four young breakfast thieves.

In my youth, I also collected and sold soft drink bottles at two cents a piece.

And I also sold cloverine salve. One day I was looking in the back of a comic book and saw an ad for cloverine salve. It said that you could sell salve and not only make big money but win terrific prizes. You could win a single-shot .22 rifle, a bicycle and, if you sold enough, even a pony.

My God, I thought, my very own pony.

I cut the coupon out and mailed it that very day. In about two weeks, my first supply of salve came back. It was a long cardboard tube and contained ten cans of cloverine salve. It also contained ten pictures of *The Last Supper,* suitable for framing. The accompanying letter said I could give away one picture with every can of salve that I sold. The letter also said that I was to sell the salve and send the money back, and then I could get more salve to sell.

I sold my first ten cans in about two days. I sent the money and sure enough, I got a new order in the mail.

I was less enthusiastic about the sales of the second batch. School had started and I was busy with my friends. Besides, I had already sold salve to all my relatives.

I didn't bother to respond to the company's first letter. It said they were disappointed in my sales results, and that if my present rate of sales continued, it was apparent that I was going to have to face the balance of my youth without the benefit of a pony.

The letter didn't bother me much, however, because it was already obvious to me that there was a glut of cloverine salve on the market. Every kid I knew was selling it. You couldn't go into any house in my neighborhood without seeing at least one picture of *The Last Supper*. Besides, my mama had already told me that if I won a pony, I'd have to keep him in my room. I didn't know a whole lot about ponies, but I knew they had disgusting personal habits that would make them impossible as roommates.

Their second letter was a little more emphatic. It indicated that I'd stolen their salve, and my heart pumped peepee. They said that prison was too good for me, and that if they didn't get either their salve or their money back, they were going to come to East Point, Georgia, and take whatever steps were necessary to protect their interest.

I remember thinking, They're coming all the way from New York to collect their $2.50. They're probably going to send a hit man. He'll shoot me down like the dog I am. Where am I going to get $2.50? It's too late to send them back their salve. I'm doomed.

I worried and fretted for days but nothing happened. I never heard from them again, and I guess if I haven't heard from them since 1944,

Making Money and Time At Glover's Pharmacy

I'm safe now.

I was fortunate enough after that to get several of what I considered to be dream jobs.

My first dream job was at the swimming pool. Somehow, I was able to talk myself into a job as a locker boy. I carried the key to all the lockers, and when the swimmers came in from the pool, they would scream, "Locker Boy! Locker Boy!" and I would go open their lockers.

I had thought a job at the pool would be real glamorous. I would get a good tan and the girls would be falling at my feet. The only problem was that I never got to see any girls in the boys' locker room. And I never even got to see the water, let alone the sunshine. It left much to be desired as a glamorous job.

My next job was at Glover's Pharmacy, where I had applied for a job as a soda jerk. It was explained to me, however, that you did not start as a soda jerk. You started as a delivery boy and worked your way up to the position of soda jerk.

A delivery boy in those days needed his own bicycle and had to be able to make change. He also needed to be willing to peddle his butt off in all kinds of weather for thirty cents an hour, plus tips. I did it for almost a year and never got a tip.

Of course, the thing that kept me going was not the money. The carrot at the end of my stick was the job as soda jerk.

I used to fantasize aloud as I was peddling up a

long hill in the rain: "Maybe when I get back, I'll find out there has been a robbery at the drug store and the soda jerk has gone down in a hail of bullets. When I get back, his bullet-riddled body will already be in the process of being embalmed at Hemperly's Funeral Home. I'll ride up on my bike and Doc Glover will say, 'OK, kid. You're our new soda jerk. Put on your uniform and start making your way in life.'"

In my fantasy, I would then go in the back room and put on my freshly starched, snow white Ike jacket. Then my clean white apron and gleaming white soda jerk cap. Then last, but not least, I would put on my black leather bow tie.

My fantasy continued with buxom cheerleader types coming in and ordering chocolate nut sundaes, slurping them down and then offering me their bodies in payment for their soda fountain bills.

That particular part of the fantasy helped me to hang in there until I finally got the job. The soda jerk didn't even die in a hold-up; his daddy made him quit when his grades plummeted.

I got my uniform and then sat back and waited for the girls to come in and throw themselves at my feet.

The first night I was there, it seemed as though my every prayer was being answered. In the front door of Glover's Pharmacy walked the most beautiful girl that had ever sucked down a fountain Coke. Not only was she beautiful and built like a brick chicken coop, she also was the head majorette at Russell High School.

What the heck if she was three years older than I was. I liked older women. Besides, only older girls knew how to appreciate a man in uniform.

As she wriggled up to the counter, I said, "Hi!"

"Hi!" she said. "Can you get me a chocolate shake?"

"My specialty," I said. Things couldn't be better, I thought. I'll make her a chocolate shake so thick she'll have to get a friend to help her chew it. Once she tastes my shake, she's mine forever. I'll quit this job and we'll run off to Daytona Beach.

Watching her drink that shake was wonderful. As a matter of fact, just watching her breathe caused most of my Presbyterian training to go right down the toilet.

She finished her shake after what seemed to be an eternity.

"Was the shake OK?" I asked.

She said it was wonderful. Then she added, "Can I say something personal to you?"

I thought, Here it comes; she's making her move. Trying to remain calm and act like Clark Gable, I said, "Sure, you can tell me anything."

She batted her eyes and said in a whisper, "If you use Noxzema every day, it'll really help your pimples. I know, 'cause my face used to look a lot worse than yours." Then she said bye-bye, swung on her penny loafers and strolled out of my life forever.

Ludlow Porch

That episode took a great deal of the romance out of my soda jerk job. I felt like my future as a lover was over. I had been to the mountaintop and the mountaintop was closed.

I had a couple of other good jobs after that. I was a lifeguard for a summer. I got a great tan and got to row a boat around the pool and blow my whistle at little kids who were running, but the harem I had hoped for was always gone when the pool closed at ten o'clock at night.

I also sold ice cream from a pushcart. That job lasted almost a full day. The cart was heavy and the money was short, and the only chance for advancement was to move up to a bigger, heavier pushcart. I passed.

Later, I worked as an usher at every movie theater in the Tri-City area. I liked that job a lot; I got to see free movies and meet a lot of girls, even if I never could sit with them. It also helped me to become a pretty fair country trivia player, which has since paid far more handsomely than the job ever did.

12

These Folks Knew How To Deliver the Goods

IN THE DAYS when not everybody had cars, delivery men were a big part of our lives. Between them and the Sears-Roebuck catalog, it was possible to never *go* shopping; all the things you wanted or needed would come to you.

Our iceman was named Robert, and he was my friend. As a matter of fact, Robert seemed to be everybody's friend. He was a tall, handsome black man, and I don't ever remember seeing him when he wasn't smiling.

Robert had a high-pitched voice and always announced his arrival by chanting in a tenor voice. He would park the ice truck, get up in the back with the ice and yell, "IIIIIICE!"

The first time I met Robert, I was about four or five years old. I had gone with the older kids to stand behind the ice truck and watch Robert chip ice. We weren't there out of curiosity; we were hoping to get a few pieces of that cool, clear treat. And Robert didn't let us down. He always made sure that there was ice left over for the children.

Robert wore a uniform that said, "Atlantic Ice and Coal" over the pocket. He also wore a leather scabbard, where he kept his ice pick. The scabbard gave him a swashbuckling air.

Robert was the only reason I was sorry we got rid of our icebox and bought a refrigerator. I'd pay dearly to hear him sing, "IIIIIIICE," one more time. And I'd tell him how much his generosity and ready smile influenced a little boy so very long ago.

Our vegetable man, Luther, was the exact opposite of Robert. He never smiled and he was a crook and a do-do. Luther would say charming little things like, "Get that wagon out of the way, boy. Somebody's gonna fall over it and get killed."

If my grandmother bought a dozen apples, Luther would go to his pickup and bring back ten in a sack. If the vegetables had to be weighed, it always came out in his favor. And when he added up the bill, he always seemed to make a small mistake to his advantage.

Any time Luther was away from the truck, I made it a point to steal something from him. Just to sort of even the score on behalf of my grandmother. I never took anything big — fruit, if he had it. If not, I took something I didn't even want, like a potato or a turnip.

That was my first venture into larceny. My conscience didn't bother me then, and as the years have gone by, I still feel OK about ripping off Luther. Robin Hood would have done no less.

The Dutch Oven man was wonderful. He came to our front door with a basket full of every goody known to mankind — doughnuts, cakes, pies and heavenly cookies.

I was grown when the Dutch Oven folks went out of business, so my childhood memories of them are unblemished. But I mourn for generations yet unborn who will never know the joy of that delightful man standing with his goodies on their front porches.

I never had much interest in the Avon lady. She didn't bring any goodies, and when you're six or seven, smelling good is pretty low on your priority list.

My mother and grandmother, however, were always glad to see her, and she seemed genuinely glad to see them. Small wonder: She always got an order. Since my mother and grandmother were such good customers, the Avon lady gave them little sample packets of good smelling stuff.

I don't remember much about the Watkins man, except that he always opened his sales pitch by giving you a little brush to clean vegetables. He carried his wares in a suitcase and sold everything from toothbrushes to furniture polish.

Ludlow Porch

The Watkins man was always very pleasant, and if my grandmother didn't need anything, he was easy to get rid of.

There were two grocery stores in my hometown that delivered — one in a Chevrolet panel truck, the other in a Cushman three-wheel motor scooter with a huge wooden box on the back for carrying groceries.

You could order a quart of milk or a whole week's worth of groceries. The goods were delivered in cardboard boxes by a smiling teen-age boy who seemed to enjoy what he was doing.

In the summertime, every fresh vegetable and fruit know to man was sold door-to-door by peddlers. There was not a set price, so customers were encouraged to haggle and to cut their best deal.

The typical conversation between my grandmother and a peddler went something like this:

"Watcha gettin' on your tomatoes?"

"Fifty cents a basket."

"I don't think so, but I appreciate you comin' by."

"Is there something wrong with them tomatoes, nice lady?"

"No, they just look a little pithy, is all. And besides, I ain't never seen no tomatoes worth fifty cents a basket. But it was nice of you to stop by. Looks like it's gonna be a hot day, don't it?"

"Yes, ma'am. It's gonna be hot all right. Nice lady, what would you give for a basket of them tomatoes?"

"Well, I don't really need that many, but I reckon I'd give twenty cents."

"Twenty cents? Ma'am, there ain't no way I could let them tomatoes go for twenty cents a basket."

"Well, you better do something, 'cause half of them is gonna be ruined by tomorrow."

"Ma'am , could you go thirty cents?"

"That's still right high, but I'll go a quarter."

"Nice lady, I can't sell them beautiful tomatoes for no quarter."

"Well, thanks for coming by anyway. I got to go. Got a cake in the oven."

"OK, nice lady, OK. A quarter. But that's one basket of tomatoes I ain't makin' a dime on."

"Watcha get on your corn?"

"Five cents an ear."

"Lawdee, ain't things high!"

And then the haggling would start all over. It was a strange way to do business, but my grandmother had turned it into an art form.

In my youth, the ultimate treat was sugar cane. It wasn't all that good, but it was hard to come by and therefore cherished. There were only two places to get it — at the Farmer's Market and from the rolling store.

The rolling store was exactly what the name implies: a big old worn-out school bus that had had all the seats taken out of the inside and replaced with shelves, vegetable bins and a soft drink box with every variety of drink ever made.

Ludlow Porch

The rolling store sold fresh yard eggs, fresh buttermilk (bring your own jar), vegetables, live chickens, candy and flower seeds. In short, the old rolling store had just about everything wonderful ever sold.

When I go into one of today's giant supermarkets, I enjoy shopping amidst all the chrome and tile. And I enjoy the push carts and the fast check-out.

In some ways I'm sorry that my grandmother didn't live to see them. It would have really been something to take her into one of those beautiful supermarkets and watch her eyes as she looked over all those fresh vegetables.

I can just hear her now saying so sweetly, "Watcha gettin' on your tomatoes?"

13

Ludlow in the Making: A Childhood Photo Album

When I was four years old, teeth were in style.

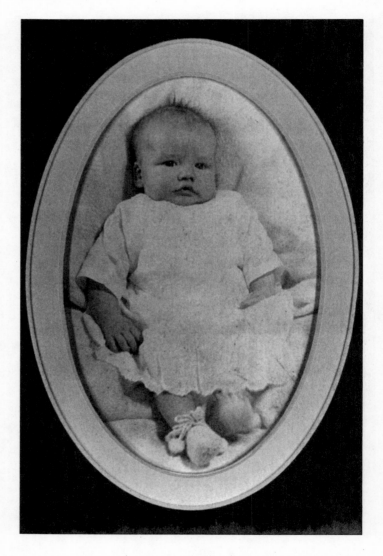

As you can see, I've been oval shaped since birth.

I supported the Navy from a very early age.

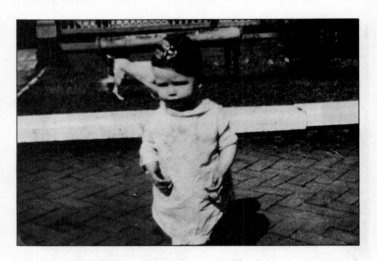

There's something about a man in uniform.

I learned about weapons at Cherokee, N.C.

Hounded by women: (L-R) Aunt Kat, my Mother,
Mama Hanson.

I'm the kid on the left . . . the one with shoes.

Storming the beach at Jacksonville, Florida.

Can you spot me in Mrs. Gurr's fifth grade class? (Back row, second from right)

Aviator caps were the height of fashion in those days.

My dog Cricket was a loyal childhood friend.

That's me and Mama at the Southeastern Fair
in Atlanta.

Ludlow Porch

My first formal portrait was made at age sixteen.

A year later, I was doing my laundry as a Marine.

14

Avoiding School Work Was Hard Work

As A CHILD growing up during World War II, I spent many happy hours in school. I also spent many hours trying to stay out of school. I would do almost anything to get out of class.

I became very interested in all grammar school activities, especially those that I knew would get me out of class from time to time. I once went to a concert by the Atlanta Symphony that I had about as much interest in as a goat has in yodeling. I sat there for two hours bored out of my little mind. My rationale was that no matter how bad it was, it beat school.

But that's a mild example of my dedication.

Every year the county offered free typhoid fever shots on a volunteer basis, and I was always first to raise my hand. Not because I feared typhoid fever, but because it would get me out of class for an hour.

Ludlow Porch

I would line up with the other medical truants, and we would walk in single file four or five blocks to the county health department, where we would stand in line and get a shot with a square needle. The shot made my arm sore for three days, but it was worth it to get out of school for an hour.

Every year we also had what was called a candy pullin'. I never knew why it was called that, because we never pulled any candy; it was already boxed and wrapped in wax paper. We took orders door-to-door for weeks before it was delivered.

I always worked my tail off at candy pullin'. I sold candy to every relative I had and to anybody else I could talk into it. The money all went to the PTA, which was a wonderful organization that did a lot of good. But when I was in the fifth grade, I didn't care two hoots about the PTA.

The reason I was so active in the candy pullin' was that you got to deliver all the candy you sold during school hours. I would be at school at nine A.M., pick up my orders and spend the day delivering them. It was a busy day, but it kept me out of school.

The same method worked for the paper sale. On a paper sale day, you took your wagon to school loaded with papers you had saved at home. After turning them in, you were paired up with a buddy and the two of you went door-to-door collecting not only newspapers but also magazines and old telephone books. The room that collected the most papers was rewarded with a party from the PTA, complete with refreshments.

Winning was wonderful. You got out of class all day for the paper sale, plus you got two more hours off for the party.

Not all of my efforts were devoted to staying out of school, however. During one period of the day it was possible to stay in school and have fun at the same time. I enjoyed recess very much.

We always did pretty much the same thing at recess. The boys started a softball game, while the girls played kickball. The afternoon in class was a little easier to take after you'd gotten a hit and stolen a base.

Another great way to stay away from long division and dangling participles was called art class. I called it playtime.

The first time I ever heard about fingerpainting was from my fourth grade teacher, Miss Freeman. I liked the idea immediately. What a thrill it was to get your hands in all that goo and not have anyone fuss at you about it.

In art class we were allowed to fingerpaint every Thursday. One day Miss Freeman was called to the office, while we were all up to our wrists in finger-paints.

Before she left the room she said, "Remember, boys and girls, I'm going to let you continue, but with every privilege there comes a responsibility."

She was no more than ten feet down the hall when we started to smear our sticky hands on one another. Apparently that did not fit within her definition of responsibility, because that was the last Thursday we ever got to fingerpaint. My budding career as a fingerpainter was over.

When I hit the seventh grade, my teacher, Miss Neese, tried to talk me into joining the Glee Club.

"No, ma'am," I said. "Only sissies sing."

"Did you know Sergeant York used to sing in his church choir?" asked Miss Neese.

"You're kidding," I said.

"It's a fact," she said.

That was good enough for me. For the next nine months I sang my guts out along with most of my buddies. I later learned that she used the Sergeant York line on all the boys and it worked every time.

But I didn't mind. It was a great way to get out of class.

15

The Holidays
Were Happy Days

EVERY HOLIDAY WAS a joy when we were growing up, but somehow Halloween, more than any of the rest, seemed to belong to us. I guess that's because grown-ups were not involved.

I should point out for the benefit of the young that "trick or treat" is a relatively new development in the celebration of this spooky holiday. Our Halloween was much less structured.

Ours usually began at school. It was no big deal — mostly the teachers hung cardboard skeletons on the walls, and we drew pictures of pumpkins with scary faces and stuck them on the windows. There was usually at least one jack-o'-lantern in each class, but that was no big deal, either, because they wouldn't let us put a candle in it.

I remember a couple of times when we had costume contests in the auditorium. Prizes were given for the scariest, the funniest and the most original costumes. The prizes usually were something like a copy of *Boys Life*, a Powerhouse candy bar or a picture of President Roosevelt, suitable for framing. Like I said, Halloween at school was no big deal. We looked forward to it not because it was fun but because it got us out of school work for at least half a day.

The real fun started after the last bell. We went home and waited for the hours to drag by until dark.

There were no wholesome activities on Halloween night. No, sir. It was a time for semi-sanctioned hell-raising. Oh, there was an occasional party with apple-bobbing and such, but for the most part it was a night for pranks.

The merchants on Main Street, for example, knew that their windows were going to get soaped on Halloween night. I never knew why it was considered so much fun to take a bar of soap and draw pictures or write names on a storefront window, but I did it anyway. I guess it was harmless enough, and it assured that all the merchants would wash their windows at least once a year.

People who owned garages made sure that their cars were locked safely inside. Window soapers loved to attack car windshields.

By the time I came along, there were not many outhouses left in town. But rest assured that we always found at least one and pushed it over. Like soaping windows, it's hard to see what pleasure we derived from pushing over some poor person's outhouse, but it seemed real important at the time. And we laughed like the little demons we were as we ran off to our next bit of mayhem.

It was about that time in my life that fire alarm boxes were introduced. When they first came out, our fire chief, Chief Wiggins, came to school and explained what they were and how to use them. He also explained, in great detail, that if anybody turned in a false fire alarm, it not only put the life of the firemen in danger, but it also took a firetruck and crew out of service, and a house could burn down while they were answering a false alarm. It made sense to me, and I was impressed by what he said.

I was more impressed, however, when he explained that turning in a false alarm was against the law, and anybody who did it would be tracked down like the gravy-sucking pig that he was. He would be found guilty by a court of law, thrown into jail for the rest of his life and then turned over to his parents, where he would be given his real punishment.

I was convinced that the last thing on earth I wanted to be involved in was a false fire alarm.

One Halloween night three of us were coming home from the movie, where we had just seen a Halloween Scream-o-Rama. That was a Frankenstein movie, one about Dracula and a new one called *The Wolfman vs. Donald O'Connor.*

As we walked past a new fire alarm, my friend Jack said, "Let's pull it and see what happens."

Ludlow Porch

"Are you crazy?" I said. "Do you know what could happen if they caught you?"

The words were barely out of my mouth when Jack pulled the lever. The box started to tick and I started to run. I was about three blocks from home at the time, but I made it to my front porch in about eight seconds. I could hear the siren blaring as I raced into the house, my heart pumping and my lungs gasping for breath.

"Did you have a good time at the picture show?" my grandmother asked.

"Yes, ma'am."

"Do you want some milk and crackers?"

"No, ma'am," I said. "I'm real sleepy. I think I'll just go on to bed."

"Do you feel OK?" she asked.

"Yes, ma'am. I'm just sleepy."

I went to my room, pulled off my clothes and jumped into bed. I was horrified. Lying there in bed, my imagination went completely out of control. They're going to have a house-to-house search, I thought. When they get here, I'll play like I'm asleep. A policeman and a fireman will break into my room screaming, "We found him, Chief. We found the little creep." Then they will drag me out of bed and off to a fate worse than summer school.

Nothing happened that night, but for the next six months I looked over my shoulder every time I saw a policeman or fireman. It was awful.

I learned a valuable lesson that night: I learned

128

what a conscience is. It's a wee small voice that whispers in your ear, "Be careful. You might get caught."

MAY DAY

Today we think of May Day as a communist holiday. We see Russians parading their tanks and missiles through Red Square.

But in the days before the Cold War got in high gear, or before it even openly existed, almost every school in this country had a May Day celebration. I was never quite sure why the other folks were celebrating. I was celebrating because there was only one more month of school before summer.

We spent all of May Day on the playground. We did folk dances, had foot races, danced around a Maypole and had refreshments, which was my personal favorite. May Day is no longer celebrated. It's just one more thing the communists have screwed up.

EASTER SUNDAY

Easter was always special for our family. It started a week before when my mother took me to Robert Hall to buy my Easter clothes. Robert Hall got all of our Easter business, I believe, because of their radio jingle. I can still hear them singing:

"Where the values go up-up-up,

And the prices go down-down-down.
Robert Hall this season,
Will show you the reason.
Low overhead, low overhead."

Easter Sunday started early for us, since we usually went somewhere to a sunrise service. Sometimes it was to Stone Mountain. Sometimes to Grant Field. If we didn't make the sunrise service, we went to our usual service at the Presbyterian Church.

Everyone there had on brand-new Easter clothes. The grown-up ladies had on new outfits with white gloves and, of course, their Easter bonnets. The men sported new suits and brand-new Wormser hats. The girls were the finest dressed of all — white shoes, white gloves and, of course, white pocketbooks. The dresses were crisp, fresh and just beautiful. All the boys wore their Robert Hall suits and their Thom McAnn shoes.

It was usually pretty chilly on Easter morning, but no matter how cold it was the girls would not put on their coats. That made sense to me. Only a complete fool would cover up all that Easter finery with a cloth coat that everybody had seen weeks before.

The church was adorned with beautiful big pots of Easter lilies everywhere. Brother Boswell had on his best black preachin' robes. The ladies in the choir all had brand-new hairdos, and they performed special Easter music.

After the service, Brother Boswell would stand outside the church door and shake everybody's hand. He would say over and over, "My, oh, my, don't you look pretty today! I love your hat. Well, don't you look like a handsome young man today. I'm glad you enjoyed the sermon. I just can't believe how much that baby has grown."

The Presbyterian Church fairly glowed with love and good will on Easter Sunday.

We left church and went straight home, where my sainted grandmother already had dinner ready. All she had to do was heat up a few things.

We ate pretty much the same thing every Easter: ham, fried chicken, potato salad, pole beans, creamed corn, lima beans, cole slaw, squash, banana pudding, rolls and sweet tea.

My granddaddy and one of my uncles would duck out during dessert, and while I was being stalled at the dinner table, they would be outside hiding Easter eggs. I knew what they were doing, but I was afraid if they found out that I knew, they would think that I was too old for an Easter egg hunt, and the fun would be over.

Finally I would get to go outside and look for eggs. I was the only grandchild at that time, so the attention was all mine. Even more important, the eggs were all mine.

Easter was a special day in my young life, and I look back on it with wonderful warm memories. To this day, I can't hear "Easter Parade" played without smelling the faint aroma of ham.

Ludlow Porch

VALENTINE'S DAY

We didn't call it Valentine's Day, but rather "Valentine."

Like Halloween, our celebration of this day usually started at school. The teacher made a huge red box with little hearts all over it and a slit in the top so we could drop our Valentines into the box.

We usually did our regular work for about half a day, went to lunch, came back to class and had our Valentine party. The Room Mother had made a cake and somebody had given us those little cinnamon hearts. If we got lucky, sometimes we even had punch.

After we had our refreshments, we gave out Valentines. They came in all shapes and sizes. There were funny ones, serious ones and, of course, comic Valentines.

The comic Valentines were not complimentary and were always signed, "Guess Who." I didn't like them much and never sent any, but looking back, some were kind of funny. One that I remember said, "New York is big and China's far, but why does your nose look like a cigar?"

If there was a girl in your class that you were sweet on, Valentine was a perfect time to let her know it without being thought a sissie or having the other boys sing, "Luddie's got a sweetheart. Luddie's got a sweetheart."

In about the sixth or seventh grade, I was hopelessly in love with Geraldine. I wasn't sure if she shared my feelings or not, but on Valentine she sent me a big heart that said, "I'd go from here to Timbuktu to get a Valentine like you."

My heart tripled in size. It was a beautiful thing and ultimately gave me the courage to ask her to go to a movie.

When school was out, we all went home and got ready for our real Valentine celebration. As the sun went down, we gathered our Valentines and started out to make our deliveries.

Once we arrived at the house, we would slip quietly onto the front porch, put our Valentines down and leave as silently as we had arrived. Once in the street, we would pick up the biggest rock we could find and throw it onto the wooden front porch.

It sounded like the world had come to an end. And, of course, we ran like crazy. I never was sure why we ran; after all, our names were signed on the Valentines. But it seemed to be the custom, and even then I was big on tradition.

NEW YEAR'S

New Year's Day was kind of a nothing holiday. We were out of school, which was nice, but we figured that was because of the Christmas holidays.

The only celebration we had occurred at midnight, but that was on the rare occasions when we were allowed to stay up late.

We would listen to the countdown on WSB

Radio, and as the man said, "five, four, three, two, one," we would run into the back yard with a pot and a big spoon, yelling, "Happy New Year!" at the top of our lungs and beating on the pot. This noisy celebration lasted for about five minutes, and then we went in and went to bed.

I told you it was a nothing holiday.

CHRISTMAS

To understand how Christmas was celebrated at our house, you must first understand a little about my grandfather. He was in charge of Christmas. He took as much time as he needed and he did it right.

He picked the tree with the loving attention of a mother hen.

We didn't have much money, but Daddy always made sure that we had loads and loads of fresh fruit. In those days, the Farmer's Market was called "Produce Row." My grandfather would come home with a huge sack of oranges, another of tangerines and still another of juicy red apples.

He would personally pick out the stick candy that was to be in dishes all over the house.

During Christmas, you didn't have to ask if you could have fruit or candy. It was a time for celebration, and it was there for the taking — as much as you wanted, whenever you wanted it.

My grandfather's personality was perfectly suited to celebrate Christmas. He stood for everything that the season represented. He was a loving, devoted husband and father. He truly believed in loving his fellow man. He respected all races and creeds and judged no man by his religion or the color of his skin, a rare trait in those days.

Some of the happiest memories of my life occurred at Christmas time. Since I was big enough to remember, I had wanted a bicycle. I had enjoyed my tricycle, but there were no sidewalks, so I was limited to the front walk of the house. Ours was only about twenty feet long. On a bicycle, however, the world would be mine. I could go almost anywhere.

I guess I was about five when my fondest wish came true. I woke up and ran into the living room, and there it was — a red bicycle. It was not new; there was no way we could have afforded a new bike. It was what they called "re-conditioned." It had fresh paint and a little metal plate on the front that said "Barry Cohen Special."

"When can I ride it?" I said.

"Right now," said my granddaddy.

"Oh, Daddy," my mother said, "he's not even dressed."

Daddy said, "No matter. You don't get a new bike every year."

Out the front door we went, me in my pajamas and my grandfather beaming that special granddaddy grin. We both had overlooked one thing: I didn't know how to ride a bicycle.

But that didn't bother either of us. He held the handlebars with one hand and the seat with the other and pushed me for about forty-five minutes. Then he said, "You ready to try it by yourself?" I was having so much fun, I was ready to try anything.

He gave me a nice soft little push and I was off. I never looked back. It was as much fun as I thought it would be. Just me and my Barry Cohen Special. That memory has to be one of my top ten.

Christmas was not only toys. It also meant my granddaddy was going to make eggnog. It meant we were going to visit Uncle Simpson and Aunt Irene and get some of my Aunt Irene's ambrosia. I never see ambrosia that I don't think about Irene and Christmas. I don't know if she invented ambrosia, but I do know that nobody ever made it any better.

Christmas will always be a special day for me, thanks to the loving folks in my family who enjoyed it as much as the children.

There were other holidays in our young lives, but I don't have many memories of them. For example, I don't have a single memory about Lincoln's birthday. We didn't even get out of school. The only memory I have of either Lincoln's or Washington's birthday was that it meant more work at school, because we had to read special stuff about both of them.

Thanksgiving was OK, but nothing to pucker over. We got two days out of school, and Lord knows the food was special, but it was more of a holiday for grown-ups than for kids. It certainly didn't hold a candle to Christmas or even Halloween. If it had not been for the two days out of school, it would hardly have been worth the bother.

16

Fred, Jr.'s Problem
Ran in the Family

FRED, JR., WAS what we called in those days a do-do. To make matters even worse, he was a second generation do-do. Both his mama and his daddy had been do-dos before him, and he even had a little sister who was a do-doette.

I think I first realized what a sorry no-account Fred, Jr., was when he told our third grade teacher, Miss Montgomery, that he loved her. Fred, Jr., always called her "Old Lady Montgomery" behind her back and said awful things about her. He was a real little hellion when she wasn't around. But let her walk into the room and he became the most syrup-mouthed little angel this side of Provo, Utah.

Some of his more famous lines to her still ring in my ears and stick in my craw:

"Miss Montgomery, Bobby's got a water pistol in his pocket."

"Miss Montgomery, do you know Jesus hears

everything we say?"

"Miss Montgomery, Sonny and Jack were playing marbles for keeps at recess."

Fred, Jr.'s great love as a third grader was to take bicycles away from smaller boys and ride them until he got tired of tormenting the defenseless children.

As an adult looking back, I don't know why we had anything to do with him at all. He should have been ostracized and treated like the little Nazi do-do that he was. But I guess children, unlike grown-ups, are more willing to overlook fatal character flaws in their peers.

Up to a point, that is.

We always played baseball at a place called the "Wood Yard." We called it that because the property was owned by the Southern Wood Preserving Company, and many years before any of us had been born they had used it as a place to store processed railroad ties.

They no longer used it for anything, and by the time we came along it was nothing more than a huge pasture in the center of heavy woods. It was a great place for kite flying and the like, but its primary use was as our ball field.

One summer day we were playing baseball there. It was one of our typical games: We had one bat, one ball and about three gloves. First base was a feed sack filled with sawdust. Second base was a rock, and third was a pine stump. Home plate was an old rusty service station sign that read, "Woco-Pep."

Some of our games would last six or seven hours, and we never kept track of anything except balls and strikes. We had no umpire, of course, and all close plays were determined by consensus. That failing, close plays were decided by fist fights.

We had been playing only about thirty minutes when Fred, Jr., tried to steal second base. He was thrown out by about fifteen feet, but he jumped to his feet and yelled, "I was safe by a mile."

We had had about all we could take from Fred, Jr., for one day, so everybody hollered at him, "Go sit down and hush. You know you're out."

But Fred, Jr., screamed back. "If you call me out, I'm gonna take my ball and go home."

Pig had taken all he could stand. He said, "Y'all hold him while I get the rope off the tire swing."

We held Fred, Jr., while Pig was getting the rope. Twit that he was, Fred, Jr., kept screaming, "I'm gonna tell. I'm gonna tell."

"Shut up," Pig said, "or I'll take this rope and we'll lynch your whinin' ass."

Fred, Jr., like all the rest of us, knew that Pig never bluffed, so he stopped whining. We took the tire swing rope and tied him to a big oak on the edge of the Wood Yard. Once this was done, we went back to our ballgame.

A couple of hours later, we got tired of playing ball and decided to play Foxes and Hounds. We had a great time.

About nine that night, I was lying on the living room floor listening to our big old floor model Philco radio when there was a knock at the front door. I didn't pay much attention to it until my mother said, "Fred, Jr.'s daddy is looking for him, Luddy. Have you seen him lately?"

"The last time I saw him, he was tied to an oak tree in the Wood Yard," I said. I could hear Fred, Sr., on the front porch shouting, "He's where? He's tied to what?"

My mother asked, "Why was he tied to a tree?"

"'Cause he said he was safe and we all knew he was out," I explained.

"What an awful thing to do," said my mother. "You should be ashamed of yourself, young man."

"It wasn't that bad," I argued. "Some of the boys wanted to burn him alive, but I wouldn't have anything to do with that."

Fred, Jr., and his family moved away not long after that. Nobody cared, because they were a real do-do family anyway. We did miss his ball, however.

17

Thou Shalt Not Steal (With Certain Notable Exceptions)

WE HAD A code of honor among the teen-age crowd that I hung out with. It was not a strict code, and we made exceptions to it every day, but for the most part we lived by it.

Under our code, it was unthinkable to steal from each other. If this was ever violated, the thief was quickly ostracized and it took him weeks to work his way back into our good graces.

It was, on the other hand, perfectly acceptable to steal from adults, especially if you stole things that were growing. It has been said many times that stolen fruit tastes much sweeter than any other kind, and from personal experience, I can testify that it's true.

The Kilgores had this magnificent plum tree in their front yard. It was not like the wild plum trees that we could find in the woods; this tree had great big old plums about the size of limes. When they were green, they were wonderful with salt, and when they were ripe, they were sweeter than a three-year-old Shirley Temple.

Both Mr. and Mrs. Kilgore liked me and would have given me all of those wonderful plums I wanted; all I had to do was ask. But I never did, because I knew that if I waited until the sun went down and snitched them, they would be much better tasting.

It never occurred to me how embarrassing it would have been had I been caught.

The same was true with peaches. In those days, I didn't even like peaches much, and peach fuzz made me itch like a yard dog in August. Nonetheless, I never missed a chance to be involved in a raid on a peach orchard.

The apex of things to steal, however, was watermelon. Every boy loved watermelon, and a watermelon raid was fun before, during and after.

I remember one raid that didn't turn out quite like I had planned. We decided on a patch to raid that was about three hundred yards off the road, just across a creek. We waited until almost dark and then sneaked into the field, each going our separate way in search of the perfect watermelon.

I could almost taste that wonderful red heart. I think that's why stolen watermelons taste best — because you can eat only the heart and throw away the rest. I found a dandy one and had broken the stem and picked it up when somebody yelled,

Thou Shalt Not Steal (With Certain Notable Exceptions)

"Run! Here he comes!"

I knew immediately who "he" was. He was the owner of the patch who wanted to take my piece of watermelon heaven away from me. I lit out for the car with my prize held tightly in my arms.

When I came to the creek, I tiptoed carefully across exposed rocks. But suddenly I hit a slick spot and fell forward right on top of my watermelon. It exploded into about ten thousand pieces.

As I lay there soaked, mourning my loss, my friends streaked past me at about forty miles an hour. The law of the land was in full effect — every man for himself — proving once again that there is no honor among thieves.

It was no problem making our getaway. My real problem was explaining to my mother why I was soaking wet and covered in watermelon from my neck to my knees.

18

Why Do Relatives Always Arrive Hungry?

MY GRANDMOTHER AND grandfather came to Atlanta from the Carolinas around the turn of the century — a young couple eager to escape the cotton mills and to start a new life.

Their brothers and sisters stayed in the Carolinas but would come to visit us from time to time. The thing I remember most about our out-of-town relatives was that they always seemed to be hungry. When they visited, my mother, grandmother and aunts seldom left the kitchen.

We never seemed to have much notice when the hungry horde was coming, either. They never called in advance, since in those days you didn't make long distance calls frivolously. They would call from the north side of town to let us know they were on the way. It never seemed to bother Mama; her main concern was that she had enough for them to eat.

She would hang up the phone and say, "OK, we've all got to pitch in. Brother and his family will be here in a couple of hours, and after that long trip from Rock Hill they're gonna be hungry."

She would go into the back yard with her apron full of chicken feed, throw some on the ground and say in a soft, soothing voice, "Chick, chick, chickie babe. Chick, chick, chickie babe."

The chickies would gather at her feet, clucking and pecking up the feed, and the whole time Mama was shopping for the nicest, fattest fryers. Once she had made her decision, her right hand would shoot out like a cobra and grab a chicken. In one motion its neck was rung and it was flopping around on the ground like a mortally wounded breakdancer.

She kept right on with her shopping: "Chick, chick, chickie babe." In short order, there were three or four chickens on the ground, their souls already departed and their remains on the way to a big black frying pan.

Inside, my aunts and my mother were cleaning and scrubbing and putting fresh sheets on all the beds. It was an unwritten law that company got the pick of the beds. We slept in whatever beds were left or on pallets on the floor.

When Uncle John and his family arrived, Mama was only minutes away from putting supper on the table. Uncle John would say, "Bessie, you shouldn't have gone to all this trouble."

Mama would answer, "It's nothing special,

John, nothing special."

I would be off in the corner watching and listening. I remember thinking, "Nothing special! God Almighty! She's killed a yard full of chickens and prepared five vegetables, plus banana pudding. If she'd fixed anymore, she would've had to buy a bigger table."

I've heard tales all my life about how the children always ate after the adults. Little Jimmy Dickens even did a song about it called, "Take an Old Cold Tater and Wait." But that was never the case at our house. The children ate first. When we had had our fill, the plates were cleaned and then and only then did the grown-ups eat. There was always plenty, anyway; after the children got through you could hardly tell any food was gone.

I've heard Mama say time after time, "These babies need their nourishment. And besides, there ain't an adult here that it would hurt to miss a meal." Of course, nobody ever missed a meal.

After supper we'd all go into the parlor and the snapshots would be brought out:

"Lawdee! I can't believe that child's grown and married."

"Don't he look precious with his cap and gown. I betcha he could make a doctor."

"John, I never seen so many good pictures. You must keep a Kodak in your hands all the time."

When it was bedtime, we found our pallets and settled in for the night. For awhile there was a lot of whispering and giggling among the children, but then a grown-up voice would say, "You children hush. It's time you were asleep. Get quiet, say your prayers and go to sleep."

The next day we would have a big breakfast, pack a lunch and go climb Stone Mountain. In a few days, the relatives from Rock Hill would leave and we'd get back to normal.

Whenever I reminisce about relatives, I always stop awhile on my Great Aunt Jill. She'd stop anybody.

Aunt Jill was my grandmother's older sister, although she went to her grave claiming that she was the "baby" of the family. Nobody is quite sure how many times Aunt Jill was married, but by the time I came along, she was wed to Uncle Red, who was at least her fourth. Uncle Red was known in carnival circles as "Ten Grand Red."

Aunt Jill was what my granddaddy called a "cutter." Any time we would hear about one of her misadventures, Daddy would chuckle, shake his head and say, "That old girl's a cutter."

She spent most of her life acquiring wealth — other people's, that is. She would steal anything that wasn't bolted to the floor, and not even her relatives were safe when her quick hands and huge pocketbook were in the area.

We had a big brass nutcracker that must have weighed eight pounds and was shaped like a bird dog. When you raised its tail, the mouth opened. Then you put a pecan in its mouth, pushed the tail down and it cracked the pecan.

One day Aunt Jill left and so did the nutcracker.

When Daddy came home, my grandmother told him. He chuckled and said, "She stole the nutcracker? Boy, that old girl's a cutter, ain't she?"

"I can't believe that Jill would steal from her own sister," said Mama.

"She'd steal from herself if she could figure out how," Daddy laughed and said. "And besides, I'd have given her that ugly old nutcracker if she'd asked for it."

I guess if Aunt Jill were alive today, society would regard her a a kleptomaniac, but we knew that she was merely a thief. Kleptomaniacs steal because they can't help it; Aunt Jill stole because she enjoyed it.

My grandmother was just too good for her own good. One time I said, "Mama, why don't you tell Aunt Jill not to steal anymore?"

"Sonny boy," she said, "you must never tell Aunt Jill that we know she steals."

"Why not, Mama?"

"'Cause it would embarrass her. And besides, if she needs it bad enough to steal it, she ought to have it."

In order to keep Aunt Jill from stealing us blind, we instituted the "Aunt Jill Alert." Whenever she would drive up, we would start hiding things that might possibly fit inside her big pocketbook. That included almost everything in the house except the bathtub. We all knew that Aunt Jill was not to be left alone even for a minute.

I remember one time she went to the bathroom and left her pocketbook unattended. My Uncle Harry took the opportunity to inspect it. She had been at our house only thirty minutes or so, and already she had a fork, one of my grandmother's aprons and a can of Dutch Cleanser. Harry took them out. When Aunt Jill came out of the bathroom, she said she had to go and left almost immediately.

We used to fantasize about what she said when she discovered her loot missing. Knowing Aunt Jill, I'm sure she said, "It's a sad day when you can't trust your own family."

In the midst of the Depression, Aunt Jill decided there was a dollar to be made in the fortunetelling business. She had a sign painted with the silhouette of an Indian on it. The sign read, *Madame Jill — Reader and Spiritual Advisor.*

When we heard about it, my grandmother said, "Oh, my Lord, this is the worst thing that has ever happened in our family."

Granddaddy just smiled and said, "That old girl's a cutter, ain't she?"

We regarded Aunt Jill's fortunetelling as a big joke. My grandmother, on the other hand, regarded it as the world's deepest, darkest secret.

One time Harry and I rode our bicycles over to Aunt Jill's house. She gave us some iced tea, and while we were sitting there, the doorbell rang.

Aunt Jill said, "Quick, go hide in the bedroom. There's a sucker at the door." She hustled us off to the bedroom and closed the door.

I turned to Harry and asked, "What's a sucker?"

"It's kinda like a customer," he said.

Aunt Jill came back into the bedroom and unscrewed a crystal ball off the post of her brass bed. She cautioned us again to be quiet and went back into her parlor.

We couldn't stand the suspense, so we listened quietly at the door. We could hear Aunt Jill talking. "Oh, yes, there is trouble in your marriage."

A man's voice said, "Yes, yes, what do you see in your crystal ball, Madame Jill?"

"I see another man. Yes, no doubt about it. Your wife is seeing another man."

"What can you tell me about him?" the man begged. "What does he look like?"

Aunt Jill peered into the bedpost and said, "That's all I can tell you for the two-dollar reading, but perhaps you would like to invest in your happiness and have a five-dollar reading."

The man was eager. "Five dollars is fine," he said.

Aunt Jill took the money and said, "I see a tall man."

The sucker interrupted. "Is he baldheaded?"

Aunt Jill, talking real low like she was in a trance, said, "I see a tall, baldheaded man."

The man interrupted again. "I knew it! I knew it! It's that son-of-a-bitch Stanley."

Never one to miss a cue, Aunt Jill said, "His

name is Stanley."

When the man asked Aunt Jill what he should do, she suggested that for ten dollars more she would tell him how to put a curse on that son-of-a-bitch Stanley.

"Yeah, that's it," he said. "I'll put a curse on him."

There was a moment of silence while he gave Aunt Jill the ten-spot. Then she started to explain. "All you do is put cursed cemetery dirt on any property Stanley owns, and after the first rain, misery, pain and loneliness will follow him for the rest of his life."

"What's cursed cemetery dirt?" asked the man.

"It's plain old dirt from any cemetery that's been cursed by someone who was born with a veil over their face."

"Do you know anyone like that?" the sucker asked.

Harry punched me in the ribs and said, "Here it comes."

"I was born with a veil over my face, and I have cemetery dirt right here," said Aunt Jill.

"Wonderful," said the man. "Can I have some?"

"Free cemetery dirt has no power," she said. "If you really want to get that Stanley, you've got to give him the full jolt, and the only way you can do that is to cross my palm with five dollars. Once you've done that, Stanley will go to bed every night cursing his mother for giving him birth."

"I only have $4.50 left," said the sucker.

"Well, give it to me and you can owe me fifty cents. I want to get that son-of-a-bitch Stanley as much as you do."

Before the man left with his fruit jar full of cemetery dirt, Aunt Jill suggested that he come back later for a love potion that would put new life into his marriage. He agreed.

I've always wondered what happened to Stanley.

I could write volumes about Uncle "Ten Grand" Red, but if I did, this book would be X-rated. You see, Uncle Red could have been captain of the U.S. Olympic cussing team.

Every child in our family learned how to cuss by simply being around him. His language could make an anvil blush. He was carny clear to the bone. He drank too much, and he and Aunt Jill were always separated. When she thought I was out of earshot, my grandmother always called Uncle Red "white trash."

I secretly liked Uncle Red, although I was apparently the only one in the family who did. I even liked the way he cussed. Let's face it: When you do something better than anyone else in the world, you should get a little respect for it.

I hope that when Uncle Red got to the pearly gates, Saint Peter took into account that he had been married to Aunt Jill. Maybe that could justify at least some of his drinking and cussing.

Aunt Jill's next husband was my Uncle Frank, a

man I loved and admired until the day he died. He was also bad to drink, but I always figured anyone married to Aunt Jill had to drink just to survive.

Uncle Frank was a fine and distinguished lawyer and was the only man on earth who could come close to controlling Aunt Jill. He tolerated her and all of her wild superstitions. Almost. The first thing he did after their marriage was insist that she stop telling fortunes. She took down her sign but still saw suckers whenever she could do so without Uncle Frank finding out.

Uncle Frank domesticated Aunt Jill to the point that they even adopted a little girl. He was trying to bring a little respectability into her life, but she fought him all the way.

One night I was visiting with them and we were playing hearts in front of Uncle Frank's huge stone fireplace. They had just bought their adopted daughter a little yipping, runny-eyed Chihuahua, and Aunt Jill had said that the dog cost fifty dollars. That was a lot of money in those days, so I decided to tease Uncle Frank.

"I never thought I'd see the day when my Uncle Frank would pay fifty dollars for a dog no bigger than a good-sized wharf rat."

He was horrified that I had accused him of such a thing. "You know there ain't never been a dog born that I'd give fifty dollars for," he said. "That blamed old dog was your Aunt Jill's idea."

Aunt Jill jumped to her own defense. "Frankie, if that dog can cure our baby's asthma, it's worth every nickel of the fifty dollars."

"Cure asthma, will it?" said Uncle Frank.

"Everybody knows that a Chihuahua can cure asthma," Aunt Jill answered.

Uncle Frank closed his cards up and turned to me like Aunt Jill wasn't in the room. "Luddy," he said, "every year our government spends millions of dollars sending missionaries to Africa to educate the heathens, and we have such vast ignorance right here in our midst."

It's a puzzle to me how they ever lived together. They were as opposite as John Wayne and Audrey Hepburn. He was the traditional old-time Southern lawyer, who was always neat and dressed like he was going to meet the president. Her hair was usually all over her head, and she dressed like she bought her clothes at a flea market. He spoke in that soft Southern drawl that most lawyers of that day used. Aunt Jill, on the other hand, was hyper in every way and especially in her speech. She spoke in bursts like a Gatling gun.

One night I was at their house for dinner. Aunt Jill was flitting about the kitchen singing, "I wish that I could shimmy like my sister Kate."

I was sitting with Uncle Frank, who had positioned himself so that he could look up from time to time to make sure that Aunt Jill wasn't burning the house down. Suddenly there was a terrible crash in the kitchen. Aunt Jill had dropped a giant economy size jar of instant coffee on the floor, and it had smashed into eighteen zillion pieces.

Ludlow Porch

Still singing, she swept the glass and coffee into a pile and poured it all through a tea strainer in a hopeless effort to remove the glass. Uncle Frank watched all this without saying a word.

In about five minutes, there was another terrible crash, even louder than the first. This time she had dropped the largest jar of peanut butter I had ever seen, and it too had shattered everywhere.

Uncle Frank looked at me over his glasses and in his best Southern drawl said, "Ludlow, if she tries to strain that peanut butter, I'm leavin'."

In legal circles, Uncle Frank was famous for his sense of humor. I always felt that was what made it possible for him and Aunt Jill to have many happy years together. She did things that would drive most men to the brink, but he seemed to take it all in good humor.

If he left a waitress two one-dollar bills as a tip, Aunt Jill would wait until he wasn't looking, pick one up and stick it in her bosom.

On the way to the car, Uncle Frank would say, "I love your cash register, Miss Jilly."

When the Lord called Uncle Frank home, Aunt Jill grieved heavily for about three hours. It wasn't that she hadn't loved him; in her way, I'm sure that she had. It was just that with his passing, she considered another chapter in her life closed, and she was ready to move on to the next one.

I'm not sure what happened when Uncle Frank reached heaven, but I like to think that Saint Peter met him with open arms and said, "Come on in, counselor. On your way up here, the Lord heard your case and the jury never left the box."

Aunt Jill, bless her soul, lived to be well into her nineties. Her last years were spent shacked up with a gentleman as old as she was. She was trying to outlive him in hopes of inheriting his money.

My granddaddy was right: That old girl was a cutter.

19

Only Our Parents Liked Prom Parties

MOST YOUNG PEOPLE today have never heard of a prom party, but they were popular events in my youth. Why, I don't know.

Boys and girls got together either at someone's house or at the school gym. There were usually refreshments and sometimes games and dancing. The girls had prom cards — little pieces of paper — on which they could write down the name of the boy who had the next promenade with them.

When it was time, the boy and girl went to walk around the block. That was the prom. Nothing else ever happened. You just walked around. Every once in a while, if you went with a girl who by our standards was oversexed, you would get to hold her hand. Otherwise, prom parties were about as dull as a Shirley Temple movie.

There were other private parties, however, where we actually played kissing games. For the younger kids, there was Post Office, but it didn't offer enough excitement for sophisticated fourteen-year-olds like us. So we modified the game and called it Pony Express. It was like Post Office but with more horsing around.

Spin the Bottle was always a crowd pleaser. It was sort of like roulette with lips. I spent hours with a dirty old Coke bottle practicing my spins, but inevitably when it came time for the real thing, my spin would end up pointing at the ugliest girl in the group. But even that wasn't bad when I was fourteen.

I guess the reason prom parties died is that kids changed. Just a few years ago it was a big deal and a pleasant experience for a boy and girl to hold hands and maybe steal a peck on the lips. Not so today, when the average American kid has his or her first sexual encounter before they're in high school.

From a parent's point of view, we ought to resurrect prom parties. We'd all sleep a lot easier.

20

The Sad Truth
About Our Love Lives

YOU HEAR MANY tales about the sexual adventures of teen-age boys, but I've got to be honest: In my day they were nonexistent.

It's not that we didn't try. And it's not that we didn't give it a lot of thought. Starting at about age fourteen, we thought of little else.

The older boys told us lies about their escapades, and we believed the lies because we wanted to. They passed on many sexual myths, like the ones about how to make a girl "hot." Once you had accomplished this, we were led to believe, many seconds of delight were sure to follow.

The method that seemed to enjoy the most popularity was putting cigarette ashes into a girl's Coke. It was common knowledge that if you did so, any girl would be "all over you." I had never had a girl all over me, but the implications were clear, and it was a prospect that certainly appealed to me.

There was, however, a serious drawback to the ashes in the Coke method: None of us smoked. We were doomed to failure before we started.

We also heard wild, outrageous tales about Spanish fly. Nobody had ever seen any, of course, and we didn't know if it was a powder, a pill, an insect or what.

We heard that it was something vets gave horses to put them "in the mood." Therefore, it was only common sense that if it would make a horse amorous, it should cause a teen-age girl to attack the nearest teen-age boy. Oh, to be the nearest teen-age boy.

Since we didn't know exactly what Spanish fly was or how to get it (we searched the shelves at the neighborhood grocery but never found any), we only fantasized and hoped that someday we might be fortunate enough to run into somebody selling this gift from Mt. Olympus. Needless to say, it never happened.

Every teen-age boy also knew that if you blew in a girl's ear, she would almost immediately fall in love and, within a matter of seconds, you could have your way with her.

I tried it once with a young girl whom I had talked into going with me to the movie. When I was sure no one would notice, I took a deep breath and blew long and softly into her ear. She turned and looked right into my sex-starved eyes. I remember thinking, What will I do if she starts to tear her clothes off right here in the movie?

Finally she spoke in a whisper. "What are you doing?"

That was the last response I was expecting. Embarrassed, I said, "I was blowing in your ear."

Unsmiling, she asked, "Why were you blowing in my ear?"

"I don't know," I stammered.

"Do you often blow into people's ears?"

"No," I said, "I swear to God, this is my first time."

"Well, stop it. It's stupid," she said.

During the rest of the movie, I gave serious consideration to becoming a priest. And that's no small decision for a fourteen-year-old Presbyterian.

My friend Herman was a source of inspiration to us all in those days. He didn't have any better luck than the rest of us, but he devoted his every waking moment to the pursuit of the fairer sex.

He started using aftershave three years before he started shaving. One day I saw him in the lobby of the movie holding hands with a girl. When she excused herself to go into the restroom, I asked, "Herman, what's that smell?"

"Old Spice," he said. "Man, if this don't turn her on, she ain't got no switches."

After the movie, Herman walked her outside where she got in the car with her mother, drove off and left poor Herman standing there on the curb. I remember thinking, There goes a ninety-eight-cent bottle of Old Spice down the drain.

Herman used to get on the trolley and ride all the way downtown just to stand on the corner and watch the telephone operators get off work. He didn't *do* anything. He just stood there and allowed his sex crazed imagination to go into overdrive. We were all envious.

When we were about fifteen, we discovered a wonderful thing — a young lady who was as interested in learning about sex as we were. I lived in constant fear that her father would find out about his daughter's horizontal activities and kill the boys involved. That same fear exists to this day, so I'll just refer to her as Mabel.

She was not a beautiful girl, but she was attractive and had what we all considered to be a wonderful attitude. She was well dressed, when she was, and gave new meaning to the word *Next*.

I don't know what ever happened to Mabel. I heard one time that she had married a soldier and moved away. I hope wherever she is that she realizes we never considered her a tart. Far from it. We always thought of her more as the Johnny Appleseed of sex.

There were certain things that all teen-age boys were expected to do. I guess nowadays you would call it peer pressure. For one, if you were a real man, you were required by the code to carry a prophylactic (a.k.a., a rubber) in your billfold.

Now, you knew when you got it that it was going to dry rot long before you were ever going to need it. But the whole idea was that it made a round impression in your billfold and all of your friends knew you had it. In fact, it was the only reason we even bothered to carry a billfold.

Not only were rubbers expensive for a teen-age budget — three for fifty cents — they also were hard to come by. Where was a fifteen-year-old going to get such a thing? The drug store? Oh, no. The druggist knew you and your family and was one of the last folks on earth you'd trust with such a deep, dark secret.

Usually you just had to bide your time and hope that someday you would walk into service station men's room and find a machine. And that on that day you had fifty cents. Those days were rare, and the machines were even rarer.

My friend Terrance was a real status seeker. He kept three rubbers taped to the underside of the dashboard in his 1940 Ford. There was, of course, no prestige to having them there if no one knew about 'em. So old Terrance told everyone who would listen about his hidden rubbers.

I always envisioned a preacher buying a used 1940 Ford off a lot, taking it home and cleaning it up and finding those same three rubbers taped under the dash. That should be fodder for a month's worth of sermons.

Ludlow Porch

Today the term sexual revolution is thrown around quite a bit. But in my teen-age years, there were a few skirmishes, no battles and certainly no revolution.

We would never "go all the way" with our steadies. We were taught that these girls were to be respected. If we were going to get lucky, it was going to have to be with a girl that we didn't care much about. That idea seemed to keep us relatively pure.

I think the real thing that slowed down our sexual activity was that in a small town, you knew most of the girls' parents. You went to church with them. You were in Boy Scouts with their brothers. It's hard to explain, but it just didn't seem like the thing to do.

Nonetheless, I never felt deprived. Mabel took care of that.

21

The Faded Glory of Drive-In Restaurants

WHEN YOU FINALLY reach that wonderful age and get your driver's license, new horizons are opened to you. Magic things start to happen. You're no longer trapped by the boundaries of your old neighborhood or the limits of your bicycle. Suddenly you can see with your own eyes places and things that until now were seen only by your older peers and later described to you over a Coke at the B & F Grill.

Most of the things described to you, of course, concerned girls.

Mother Nature is a right smart old girl, and her timing on such matters is about perfect. When a young man's interest in girls peaks, Mother Nature makes him old enough to be able to drive. Shortly thereafter he learns that one of the best places to meet new girls is drive-in restaurants.

It therefore becomes a ritual for a carload of boys

to go to a drive-in and cruise around the parking lot until they find a carload of girls. They then strike up a conversation, hoping to come away with at least a telephone number.

The most popular drive-in we haunted was the Varsity. It was advertised as the world's largest drive-in. We surmised that if it was the biggest, it would attract the most girls. We were right; it was a rare night, indeed, when we failed to meet a new girl at the Varsity. I was twenty-six years old before I knew they served food there.

In those days, the majority of customers at the Varsity ate in their cars. When you pulled in, a smiling black man put a number on your car and jumped on the running board or trunk lid and rode with you to find a parking place.

If you were lucky, your curb hop was Flossie Mae, an older black man who wore outrageous flower-filled hats and sang the menu:

"We got hamburgers, cheeseburgers, lettuce and tomato,
Boiled ham, baked ham, and French fried potatoes."

The Varsity was the most famous drive-in but certainly not the only one. They were everywhere. Some were good for eating; others were best for devilment.

There was one close to home called the Polka Dot Drive-In. The curb boys there had the annoying habit of jumping onthe running board while the car was still moving, sticking their heads inside the car and screaming, "Park it right over there."

One night after a movie, we decided to go to the Polka Dot for a hot dog and a Coke. We were in Floyd's 1938 Chevrolet with him driving, Pig in the passenger's seat and me in the back.

We pulled into the Polka Dot and immediately the curb hop came sprinting up, jumped on the running board, stuck his head in Pig's face and shouted, "Park it right over there." In one motion, Pig rolled the window up tight on his neck. Floyd threw the Chevy into second gear, made a U-turn with tires smoking and raced back into the street.

In seconds, we were up to about fifty miles an hour, and the curb hop was begging us to stop.

"Shut up," said Pig. "We're gonna kill you."

The curb hop kept pleading. "Lawd Gawd, please stop. Please don't kill me. Why would you want to do that?"

"'Cause you never bring enough ketchup for the French fries," said Pig.

The hop started crying. "Lawd Gawd, Mr. Pig, you can't kill a man for not bringin' enough ketchup."

"Sure I can," answered Pig. "I once killed a man 'cause he was Methodist. If we don't kill you, do you swear to bring enough ketchup next time?"

"Yes, God, I swear it. I'll bring you ten gallons of ketchup if you want it," said the hop.

Pig made him swear it before telling Floyd to

stop the car. Then he rolled down the window and released the poor hop. We drove off like three crazy men, leaving the hop standing on the side of the street screaming, "I'm gonna have y'all put in jail for kidnapping."

I don't know why we didn't go to jail. Lord knows, we deserved it.

Unfortunately, most of the drive-ins are gone. I guess the fast food places dealt them a mortal blow. What a shame, because also gone forever are great names like the Yellow Jacket, the Blue Jacket, the Snack Shack, Campbell's and Arthur's.

I know there are other places for young boys to meet girls nowadays, but where do they go to steal glasses?

22

Ford vs. Chevrolet: It Was War on Wheels

WHEN I WAS a teen-ager, there were basically only two kinds of men: those who drove Fords and those who drove Chevrolets. They were referred to, of course, as Ford men and Chevy men.

In those days it was generally accepted that Plymouth was an "off brand," Nash should have stuck to making ice boxes (Kelvinator), and driving a Studebaker was like wetting the bed — you weren't blamed for it, but at the same time you were expected to feel ashamed.

Most small Southern towns had a Ford dealership and a Chevrolet dealership. The population was split pretty much down the middle with violent opinions about which was the best car. I have actually seen grown men almost come to blows as they discussed the best make.

The argument usually started with a small barb: "Is that a Chevrolet you're drivin'? I had a

Chevrolet one time. Worst car I ever had. Wouldn't pull a sick whore off a slop jar."

"Oh, yeah? I'd rather have a sister workin' in a cathouse than a brother drivin' a Ford."

It was at about this point that a neutral bystander would interrupt and say, "Come on, guys, you're arguing about something silly."

Then he got it from both sides. "Silly? Silly? What do you know, you dumb ass? You drive a DeSoto. I'd rather have a social disease than be in the same used car lot with a DeSoto."

There was usually a gentleman in the crowd who would have the last word on any subject. He would take a long drag on his Tampa Nugget, blow smoke into the air and say softly, "I'd rather walk through a chicken house barefooted carryin' a Chevrolet hubcap than own the best Ford ever made."

Nobody could top that one.

23

A Good Chicken
Is a Fried Chicken

I **HAVE FOUGHT** the battle of the midriff most of my adult life. I can walk within three feet of a piece of pecan pie and gain fourteen pounds.

I have long since discovered that my problem is not the amount of food I eat but rather *what* I eat. My taste buds have decided on their own that the kind of food I grew up on is the only kind they'll gracefully accept.

In my family, we ate food that was (1) not too expensive, and (2) that would stick to your ribs or anything else it touched.

Eating patterns are established early in life. I think my fate as a fat person was sealed the first time somebody stuck a mashed-up butterbean into my little baby mouth. By some standards, folks might say that I led a nutritionally depraved childhood, but that's not so. We just ate the typical Southern fare of the day and never ventured out into the cuisine of our northern brothers.

I never saw broccoli until I was an adult. I knew it existed, because I had read something about it in *My Weekly Reader*. The same was true of Brussels sprouts. They were not served at home or at school or even on our infrequent visits to restaurants.

And we never ate salads. I guess the closest we came was sliced pineapple on lettuce with a spoonful of mayonnaise and some grated cheese on top. We ate all the ingredients of salads, but we ate them separately. When tomatoes were in season, for example, we ate them three times a day (a divine habit that continues with me till this day).

We also ate a lot of cucumbers, either raw and lightly salted or soaked in vinegar but not mixed up with lettuce. We did eat lettuce from time to time, but only on a sandwich.

My distaste for a traditional salad continues today; I'd rather have my car greased than eat one. When I go out to dinner, I have no desire to graze. I'm there to eat meat and bread and starch. Especially starch.

The meats we ate were almost always fried. The only exceptions to this were the Thanksgiving turkey and meatloaf. That was pretty much it. I was grown before I knew you could have chicken any way except fried.

My prejudice for fried chicken has stayed with me; I mistrust anyone who tries to bake a chicken. I believe in-depth research would show that these people have criminal tendencies, are not close to

Jesus and have either dead or inactive taste buds.

The vegetables of my childhood were a thing to behold: corn fixed seventeen different ways; every type of bean ever picked; black-eyed peas; every kind of potato fixed every way you could imagine — mashed, fried, boiled and baked, and sweet potatoes baked with a big dob of cow butter right in the middle; and sweet potato pies for special occasions like Christmas and Thanksgiving.

And bread. Ah, the bread. Homemade biscuits, cornbread, hot rolls and sometimes fresh loaf bread for sandwiches.

I could write an entire chapter about the desserts, and I would start it with my grandmother's fried pies. They were little half-moon delights that rarely lasted more than about ten minutes after they came out of the pan.

Next I would write about blackberry cobbler, made from blackberries that we had picked and washed just hours before the cobbler was baked. And the same with apple and peach cobbler. And my favorite of all was banana pudding — thick, rich and full of bananas and vanilla wafers.

Of course, no discussion of childhood desserts would be complete without mentioning the ice cream that we made in our own freezer. In the South of my youth, every family had a member who was the expert on homemade ice cream. In our family, that person was my Uncle Chuck.

He could make all flavors, but like all great ice cream makers down through the ages, he had a specialty: Uncle Chuck made the best peach ice cream ever churned.

To make perfect peach ice cream, you must have four things: (1) peaches at just the right stage of maturity, (2) a good, dependable ice cream freezer, (3) the perfect recipe, (4) and Uncle Chuck. Anything less and you're doomed to fall short of perfection.

I'm sure that if I had been raised in a family that ate more salads and less starch, more honey and less sorghum syrup, more wheat bread and fewer cathead biscuits, I probably never would have had to go on so many diets.

But I also wouldn't have had half as many wonderful memories of eating. Did you ever hear of anybody writing a book about growing up eating broccoli? I rest my case.

24

The New Way of Talking Ain't Worth Doodley Squat

WHEN I WAS a little boy, the language was different. It was still English, but it seemed to have more color and it certainly was more regional in nature.

If you asked someone how he felt, more than likely he would reply, "Tolable." Not tolerable, "tolable." It was mispronounced but we all knew what it meant. When someone was "tolable," it meant that he was able to sit up and take nourishment but not able to go to work.

Feeling "puny" meant that you were a little worse than "tolable" but not quite sick.

"Bilious" was a term used when everybody agreed that you were not well, but nobody was exactly sure what was wrong with you.

"Pekid" meant that you had changed color, usually from your normal color to a shade of light green.

Ludlow Porch

If you were "down in your back," it meant you were unable to move about.

When you were "stove up," it could mean a number of things were wrong: "He's all stove up with the flu," or, "He fell out of the loft and now he's all stove up," for example.

If you listened carefully to two old biddies talking about the town drunk, the conversation would go something like this:

"Have you heard the latest about Leon?"

"Naw, what?"

"Well, you know he's bad to drink."

"Bad to drink ain't half of it. He stays loop-legged most of the time."

"Lawdee, ain't that the Gospel. Well, for the past two weeks he's been in Atlanta laid up with an old woman."

"I swan. Bless his poor mama's heart."

"He don't care nothin' 'bout his mama. Treats her like a red-headed stepchild."

"He ain't never been worth doodley squat."

"He's the kind of old liquor head that the Ku Klucks ought to get."

"Amen to that, sister. Amen to that."

"He ain't worth shucks."

"I do feel sorry for his mama, though. Makes me want to clabber up and cry every time I think about the way he's done her."

"He never was that way before the Army sent him across the water."

"Yeah, but since he got back, he ain't missed a juke joint between here and Tyler, Texas."

"Yeah, ever since the Army turned him out, he's looked right funny out of his eyes."

I would guess that if you lived north of Richmond, it would have been very hard to carry on a conversation with any of us from the Deep South.

The weather has always been of great importance to Southerners. I suspect that comes from generations of living off the land when your prosperity was left entirely to Mother Nature and her whims. The weather, therefore, has been the topic of many colloquial expressions:

"Looks like it's comin' up a cloud, don't it?"

"Lawd God, I hope so. My pasture's so dry the cows have gone to totin' canteens."

"That cloud's comin' down Jack's Creek, and that generally means we're gonna get a real gully washer. I wouldn't care if it drowned ever' duck in the county."

There was also much talk about the cold weather:

"You reckon it's gonna snow?"

"I hope so. If it gets deep enough, that dang boll weevil might just go to hell, back to Mexico."

"You remember that snow we had here in '38?"

"Do I remember? It was waist deep on a tall Indian. Out at my place, you had to stand on a tall corner post to pee. And cold! I ain't never seen it so cold. Old Rube's house got so cold one night that when he got ready to blow out the candle in his bedroom, the flame was froze solid."

"You're puttin' the shuck on me."

"Naw, it's the Lord's truth. And that ain't all. You know Rube can't sleep when there's light in the room, so he took out his pocket knife and cut the flame off that candle and throwed it out the window. Well, along about first light, it warmed up a little and that flame thawed and, Bless Pat, it burned Rube's house slap to the ground."

"You're the biggest liar in these counties. You'd rather climb a tree and tell a lie than stand on the ground and tell the truth. Man alive, are you a liar. I bet you got to get somebody else to call your dogs."

Saying hello and good-bye in the South has always taken a little time to do properly.

When I was a little boy, I would often be stopped on the street by the old men. Today we call them senior citizens, but we called them old men; nobody seemed to mind and certainly no disrespect was intended.

The conversation would start when the old man asked, "Whose boy are you?"

When I told him, he always said, "Lawd God, boy. I knew your granddaddy."

When we parted, he would say, "Boy, when you get home you tell your mama that Old Man Singleton said hidee."

If you ran into somebody you hadn't seen in a while, the greeting was, "Howsyourmamaanem?"

You always said, "Fine, thanks, 'n' yours?" You

always answered fine, even if your mama was dead.

When company left the house, you could say a number of things, including, "Come see us, now," or, "Y'all come back," or, "Hold it in the road," or, "Keep it 'tween the ditches," or, "Hold 'er in the ruts," or, "Don't stay gone so long."

We also had very colorful ways of describing a person's physical appearance:

"She's so bowlegged she couldn't hem a hog up in a ditch."

"They had such ugly children that when they made home movies, they hired stand-ins."

"Looks like her face caught fire and somebody beat it out with a shovel."

"When he was little, he was so ugly that his mama used to tie a pork chop around his neck so the dogs would play with him."

"He's as ugly as homemade sin."

"She's so ugly she could make a freight train take a dirt road."

"Boy, is she ugly! She could knock a buzzard off a gut wagon."

"Look at that nose. Betcha that old boy could smoke a cigar in a rainstorm."

"That old boy sure has got funny lookin' ears. Look like jug handles, don't they?"

"His face would stop an eight-day clock."

"He'd make a go-rilla gag."

There were also colorful ways to describe skinny

people:

"He's so skinny he has to run around in the showerbath to get wet."

"He's so skinny that I betcha he could get into his T-shirt from either end."

"That's girl's so skinny that if she swallowed an olive, nine guys would leave town."

"Lawd, ain't she skinny. A good stout wind would blow her slap away."

And there were special ways to describe some with a bad temper:

"He's meaner than an ingrown toenail."

"I betcha he'd fight a circle saw."

"He's so ill-tempered he'd fight Pharaoh's army."

There were literally hundreds of other colorful phrases. For example, a place where you could dance and drink was called a "juke joint." People on their way to a juke joint were said to be "goin' jukin'."

If you had been attacked by another boy, you said, "He jumped on me."

Kissing a girl was called "smoochin'."

When a girl left home on a date and her mother was worried about how honorable the boy's intentions were, she would always tell her daughter, "Don't let that old boy mess with you."

People who wouldn't work were called "sorry." If they wouldn't work and also had a drinking problem, they were said to be, "sorry and no account."

A boy who was a sharp dresser was known as "a

dog in the road."

A girl who could cook, make good grades in school and played "Root the Peg" was not called versatile; she was referred to as "a good old girl." Also, a girl you could cuss in front of without her telling on you was called "a good old girl."

If something made you mad, you said, "It just didn't sit well with me."

If you were tired, you were "whooped," "wore out" or "all tuckered out." Or, if you were exhausted, you were "pass goin'."

If you thought a joke was funny, you said, "That flat tears me out of the frame."

If you wanted to tell a small child that something he had done was funny or cute, you simply said, "You're a mess, boy."

If you wanted to say thank-you to someone, you said, "'Preciate it," or, "Much obliged."

Bicycles were called "wheels," as in, "Don't you fall off that wheel and break your neck." Tricycles were called "trikes," and stilts were called "Tom Walkers."

Halloween masks were called "dough faces," and a baseball catcher was always referred to as a "hind catcher."

An overweight person was said to be "kinda stout."

If you were hammering a nail and hit your finger, there were several socially acceptable things you could say: "Confound it!" or, "Doggone it!" or, "Son of a gun!" or, "Son of a seacook!" or,

Ludlow Porch

"God bless America!"

If your mother called you home, you would answer by screaming, "Comin'!" That meant you were on the way. Or, you could say, "I'll be there tareckly (directly)." That meant you would be there as soon as you gathered up the lead soldiers you were playing with.

A "grass widow" was a divorced lady. A lady whose husband had actually died was referred to as a "poor old widder woman."

Any child whose parents had died was called "that poor little orphan child."

If someone was doing well financially, you would say that he was making "right smart."

It wasn't just the phrases which were colorful in my youth. Single words themselves seemed to be more fun and more expressive, or at least clearer. For example, take the following list of words used then and now:

THEN	NOW
soda crackers	saltines
dinner	lunch
supper	dinner
curtains	window treatments
rugs	carpets
sneakers	tennis shoes
running naked	streaking
Kodak	camera

The New Way of Talking Ain't Worth Doodley Squat

THEN	NOW
constipation	irregularity
settee	love seat
davenport	sofa
overalls	jumpsuit
linoleum	floor covering
parlor	great room
navel	belly button
haircut	styling
ear bobs	earrings
spy glasses	binoculars
Victrola	stereo
liquor head	alcoholic
dope fiend	drug abuser
shackin' up	cohabitating
poor	underprivileged
smut	pornography
funnies	comic strips
chapped	chafed
fat	full-figured
crazy	emotionally disturbed
weenie	frankfurter
loaf bread	bread
sweet milk	milk
with ice	on the rocks
blind	visually impaired
queer	gay
false teeth	dentures
Dagwood sandwich	club sandwich
roastin' ear	corn

Ludlow Porch

THEN	NOW
hunkie	Eskimo Pie
little bitty	mini
movies	films
Co-Cola	soft drink
Frigidaire	refrigerator
Mix Master	mixer
appetizers	hors d'oeuvres

The list could go on and on, but the point is that the language has definitely changed. I'm not suggesting that the way we talked was good or proper, but I do believe it made my childhood more colorful and therefore more pleasant.

We always knew what we were saying and, with apologies to the folks at Harvard and their kind, it was by-god good enough for us. And I miss it.

25

These Were a Few
Of My Favorite Things

I OFTEN MARVEL at the fact that the world continues to turn without the help of Price Albert tobacco cans. When I was a child, it was common knowledge that an empty Prince Albert can was about the most useful thing a child could have.

It was shaped to fit into a pocket and perfect for keeping personal treasures in — a picture that a certain little girl had given you, a rusty knife or the combination to your bicycle lock, for example.

You could also keep your best marbles hidden away there from the rest of the world. And if you liked to fish, your Prince Albert can would hold several hooks, fishin' line wrapped around a stick, several sinkers and at least one cork.

The list of possible uses was almost endless, but the thing I used mine mostly for was a crawfish trap.

There was a dandy little creek less than a hundred yards from our house that held more wonders for a small child than Mark Twain's Mississippi, and the best of these were crawfish.

The first thing you needed to know to become a successful crawfish hunter was that crawfish swim backwards. I'm sure that the crawfish thinks it's forward, but then and now I consider it backwards.

With this in mind, you took your Prince Albert can and walked the bank of the creek till you spotted a great big old crawfish. Then very carefully you put the Prince Albert can in the water directly behind the crawfish. Once this was done, you put your other hand in the water right in front of the unsuspecting crustacean and wiggled your fingers. The startled crawfish would back right into the Prince Albert can. You slammed the lid shut and he was yours.

If I didn't feel like getting wet, I put aside my Prince Albert can and spent hours catching and playing with June bugs. What a marvelous little creature.

I never knew for sure exactly what they were — some sort of beetle, I suppose — but they were beautiful, plentiful, harmless and great fun.

They had large, fat legs, and it was relatively easy to tie a long piece of thread around one of their legs. You would then hold the other end of the string and let the little darling go. He would fly in circles 'round and 'round your head. It was great fun, and somehow you knew that the June bug enjoyed it almost as much as you did.

Lightning bugs were another matter. They were good for only one thing. Once you caught them, you put them in a jelly jar, but only after you had punched holes in the top with an ice pick.

Then you just looked at them. That's all.

When you went in the house, you generally left your lightning bugs and jelly jar on the front porch. When you went out the next morning, they were all dead.

Looking back on it, it seems like a waste of a good jelly jar.

Turtles were a lot more fun and one of my special things. I regarded turtles as very special creatures and studied them by the hour. After a day or two, I was careful to turn them loose down near the creek.

Sometimes I would paint my initials on their backs before I set them free. I never found one with my initials, but I'm still looking.

Next to a Prince Albert can, the best thing a little boy could own was a cigar box. It was like your own private strongbox. You could keep all of your old pencils and color crayons and all the other special things in your life in it.

If you wanted to insure absolute privacy, you simply drew a skull and crossbones on the lid of the cigar box and wrote under it, "Keep out! This means you." You knew that only a real do-do would dare to violate your privacy.

Ludlow Porch

New shoes were a big deal when I was growing up. The only time new shoes came your way was when the old ones had been half-soled and heeled about three times.

Even after you got new shoes, you couldn't wear them whenever you wanted to. The new shoes became "Sunday shoes" and were reserved for Sunday school, church, weddings, funerals and graduations. Your old "Sunday shoes" became your "everyday shoes" whenever you bought a new pair.

Once I hit the seventh grade, Thom McAnn shoes became one of my special things. Not just any of Thom's shoes, but a special kind of shoe: the black, plain-toe, navy-style shoe. I was absolutely convinced that this was the most handsome footwear a twelve-year-old boy could possibly wear.

They cost five dollars, and it was a great day, indeed, when my mother sent me after those new shoes. I would get on the trackless trolley in East Point, Georgia, ride it to downtown Atlanta to Rich's, walk to Five Points and there it was: Thom McAnn's.

I would try them on until I found just the right pair. Then the salesman would say, "Do you want to wear them?" "Yes sir," I said. "I'll wear them."

He would put my old shoes in a box and I'd start for home. I was sure that everybody I passed on the street was staring at my new shoes and thinking, "My, oh, my. Doesn't that young man have on beautiful shoes?"

Another of my favorite things when I was a boy was homemade lemonade. If you want lemonade today, you just pop a top on a frozen can and in about three minutes you're drinking lemonade. It doesn't taste much like real lemonade, but the label on the can assures you that it is.

Real lemonade was one of my granddaddy's favorite projects. It was usually a Sunday after-church project, and he made it into a major production.

Granddaddy would get out a big punch bowl, put it on our kitchen table and then cut lemon after lemon in half and squeeze them into the punch bowl. The cutting and squeezing were done with a great deal of flair.

Once the lemon juice was squeezed, it was time to add the water and the sugar. Then and only then was the cracked ice added. Once the ice was added, it was stirred and stirred.

The whole time it was being made, I would stand beside the table in big-eyed anticipation. When it had been stirred for what seemed to me like an eternity, my granddaddy would turn to me and say, "Are you ready for the test?"

"Yes sir, Daddy. I'm ready."

He would give me a spoonful and say, "What do you think, big boy?"

I would always say the same thing. "It needs more sugar, Daddy, more sugar."

He'd smile and say, "OK, you're the boss. You're my lemonade expert."

Ludlow Porch

He would then add sugar and let me taste it again. Once it was pronounced perfect, we carried the whole punch bowl to the front porch, where we all sat around and sipped on our lemonade. The grown-ups read the Sunday paper and we kids listened to the radio and sucked down the most wonderful lemonade ever made.

I don't expect anyone under forty to appreciate this, but making lemonade was a big deal to us, and it sure beat the devil out of Minute Maid.

Watermelon was also a big deal in my childhood. We didn't have it often, but when we did my granddaddy made sure it was a melon to remember. It always happened on Sunday under a huge oak tree in our back yard.

After it had sat in a cool spot most of the day, my granddaddy would bring out the melon and take great pains in cutting it into wedges. This was a production of great importance and could not be rushed. For some reason, the watermelons of my memory seem colder, riper and had fewer seeds than today's.

If you haven't gotten the idea by now, Sunday was a special day in my childhood. In the springtime we would get out of church about noon and go right home for one of my grandmother's famous Sunday dinners.

Afterwards, when everybody else was sittin' around readin' the newspaper and listenin' to the radio, Granddaddy would say to me, "You know what would be good about now?"

"What?"

"Some ice cream."

"Ice cream would be great," I'd say.

"Well, why don't we walk up to the drugstore and see if old Doc Glover would sell us some of his ice cream?"

Then we'd walk off up Spring Street holding hands, an old man smoking a little stump of a cigar and a five-year-old who loved him with all of his heart.

Glover's Pharmacy had double doors and, weather permitting, they were always propped open. This allowed the fresh air to come in so the overhead fans could pick it up and spread it all over the interior of the soda fountain area.

There was a marble-topped counter complete with spotless chrome fixtures.

There was a big mirror behind the fountain, and written on the mirror in red letters was, "Fountain Coca-Cola Served Here." Under that in real fancy letters was, "The Pause That Refreshes."

The soda jerk's name was Forest, and he had on a snow-white uniform and he smiled the whole time we were there.

Once we each had our ice cream cone, the walk home started. It was very slow because we planned it that way. We didn't want to get home too soon. This was our special time together, and we savored each step almost as much as we did old Doc

Glover's ice cream.

The park was right on our way home. We would stop and Granddaddy would swing me for a while. Then he would say, "We better head for the house now, Bocephus, or your grandmama's gone skin us both."

"Just ten more times, Daddy. Just ten more times."

"Okey-dokey. Ten more times, then we're goin' home."

"Daddy, when we get home, will you read me the Sunday funnies?"

"Boy, you know you don't like for me to read you the funnies."

"Yes I do, Daddy. I promise I do."

My granddaddy died two months after my seventh birthday, but has lived on in my thoughts. I think about him every time I get a whiff of cigar smoke in the air or taste real lemonade or read the Sunday funnies. It's impossible to forget someone that you loved as I loved him.

There were many precious things around in my childhood that I took for granted. Then one day I noticed that they were gone. They're no big things taken as individual items, but as a group they represent something else that is also gone — my childhood.

GOURD DIPPERS: Like everyone else who ever had a drink of well water out of a gourd dipper, I knew that it was special. I have never been able to understand why anyone would drink water out of anything else.

Why are the kitchen cabinets of America full of glasses when one gourd dipper per family could put them in the water-drinking business and make them the envy of the crowned heads of Europe?

FORTUNETELLERS: Just a few short years ago, the countryside abounded with fortunetellers. It was almost impossible to ride ten miles in any direction without seeing one of their signs. There were two kinds of signs. One was the outline of an Indian's head, complete with war bonnet. It read, *Madame Zelda* or *Sister Marie — Indian advisor and healer.* The other kind of sign was the outline of a hand. It said, *Madame Zelda* or *Sister Marie — Palmist and Reader, knows all, sees all, tells all.*

Parked close to the sign was a house trailer. The inside of the trailer was decorated in early midway, and it looked like everything in it had been won at the carnival.

The fortuneteller wore bright clothes and a shawl, and most times she held a Chihuahua dog or two that had runny eyes.

Everything in the trailer had red ball fringe — the sofa, the chair, her shawl and even the Chihuahuas.

She was always married to a gravy-suckin' pig, who was too sorry to work. His main function in life seemed to be to help her hold one of those little runny-eyed, yappin' dogs.

The husband was always tall and skinny and reminded me of Henry Fonda in *The Grapes of Wrath*.

One day I looked up and the fortunetellers were gone. In their places today we have people who call themselves psychics. They don't work out of trailers. They don't even put up those great signs. But I betcha if you searched their houses, you could still find some red ball fringe.

TOWN DRUNKS: There was a time when almost every small town had its very own drunk. He was usually an old boy who had toyed with drinking for a number of years and knew that he enjoyed drinking better than almost anything else.

Then one day he found out that the old town drunk had either died, gone to jail or left town. He was tickled to death to learn that there was an opening for a new town drunk.

He also knew that if he was to take over the position of acknowledged town drunk, that he would have to stop any pretense of work. Being a town drunk is a full-time job. The only time you're allowed to do any work is when you're so broke you can't buy any booze.

When that happens, it's OK to get you a job painting a house. The only stipulation is that as soon as you earn enough money to get blind, stinking, fallin' down drunk, you have to return to being the town drunk.

Today they call 'em alcoholics and winos, and they try to dry 'em out in special hospitals or put them in jail.

Sometimes we pay an awful price in the name of progress.

WRINGER WASHING MACHINES: I'm sure that no woman on the face of the earth misses the old wringer-type washing machine. I don't see how they could. It took all day to accomplish what you do now by pushing about four buttons.

On the other hand, it's easy for me to stay nostalgic about that old relic since I never had to use it.

Somehow, when I woke up and heard our washing machine, I knew that all was well at our house. That meant my mother and grandmother had brought the washing machine off the back porch and into the kitchen, and it was making that wonderful sound — *ka-jung, ka-jung, ka-jung.*

Sometimes I was allowed to help. My job was to catch the clothes as they came out of the wringer and make sure they went into the large wicker basket so they could be carried out and hung on the clothesline.

I know how much trouble and work the old washer and clothesline were, but somehow when you got between those clean, fresh-dried sheets at night, it was all worth it. Seems to me that there's never been a dryer that worked as well as the one the Lord gave us.

Ludlow Porch

HEROES: Heroes used to be important, and every child I knew had his favorite. In my neck of the woods, President Roosevelt was everybody's hero. You never ever heard one word against him. I didn't know anything about politics, but I heard all the grown-ups talk about what he had done for the country by whippin' Hoover and stopping the Depression.

I was convinced that being a Republican was worse than being a child molester.

I didn't know anyone who claimed to belong to the Grand Old Party, but I had heard the grown-ups talk about Wendell Wilkie, and I knew that if he beat Roosevelt, we'd be living in caves in less than thirty days.

We stayed up late that election night of 1939 and listened to the returns come in on the radio.

Then we got up early to see if it was official. It was; Roosevelt had beaten Wilkie like he'd just stolen a government check.

The same was true when Tom Dewey had the gall to run against our beloved FDR. I remember the old men talking about Dewey. They said things like:

"Look at that little weasel. He's got enough oil in his hair to grease the back axle of a John Deere tractor."

"You can just look at him and tell he's a crook, can't you?"

I couldn't figure out how any politician in the country could have the nerve to run against President Roosevelt. You could just listen to him on the radio and know that he was a great man. Didn't he make the Depression go away? Didn't he tell the Japanese and Germans that he was going to wear 'em out? Didn't he come to Georgia on a regular basis? Yes, sir! In the Deep South, President Roosevelt was a hero to children and grown-ups alike.

Funny thing — none of the grown-ups liked Eleanor, but they didn't talk bad about her much because of their respect for the president.

Joe Louis was another of my heroes. He was quiet, modest and loved his country. I still remember his great quote as he went into the army: "We will win, 'cause God is on our side."

Joe was not as popular with some of my young friends as he was with me. They didn't like him much 'cause every year he beat up two or three white men. I handled this by telling myself that I was sure he meant no disrespect.

A lot of my friends had General MacArthur as a hero, but I didn't like him much. I don't know why; I guess it was because he never smiled. He reminded me of the stern, strict schoolteachers that I had heard about.

I just knew that if any of his troops did anything wrong he would either make them stand in a corner or take a hickory stick and "switch 'em good."

I was a big reader of the comic books, and many of my heroes came from there. Captain Marvel was one of my favorites. I especially liked him because he was the alter ego of a boy named Billy Batson. When Billy got into trouble or needed to stomp a mud hole in a crook, all he had to do was say "Shazam," the magic word. Lightning would come down and strike the ground with a deafening crash and a great deal of smoke. When the smoke cleared, Billy Batson was gone and, lo and behold, there stood Captain Marvel, ready to right the wrongs of the world. He wore a red bodysuit with calf-length gold boots, a gold lightning bolt across his chest and a gold cape. He could fly and was bulletproof. He was something else.

A lot of my friends liked Superman better than Captain Marvel, but I was always a little suspect of "The Man of Steel." I didn't understand why folks couldn't tell that he was really Clark Kent. All he did was put on a pair of black, horn-rimmed glasses, and nobody could tell who he was. I didn't understand it then and I don't understand it now.

Mandrake the Magician was also one of my heroes. He could hypnotize folks in the flash of an eye. If a crook was holding a gun on him, he would gesture hypnotically and make the bad guy think the gun was a snake or a chili dog. Mandrake was nearly invincible.

He had a beautiful girl who was his friend and assistant. He also hung around with a giant black guy named Lothor. When you got Mandrake and Lothor together, they could handle anything from Nazi spies to gangsters.

Mandrake was also the sharpest dresser in the comic books. I read his adventures for all of my childhood and never saw him dressed in anything but a tuxedo. It seems strange to me now, but I thought at the time, "That Mandrake, he's one sharp dressing son of a gun."

The movie cowboys were all my heroes to one degree or another.

I liked Randolph Scott and Johnny Mack Brown best because they had Southern accents. When I was nine or ten, I became a big Bob Steele fan. Bob Steele was the shortest cowboy in the movies. I think I liked him because he wasn't much bigger than me, but he was one fightin' hombre. He would whip three or four bad guys just for the exercise. He was so short that he had some trouble getting on a horse, but that didn't matter to me, I sure did like old Bob Steele.

Strange as it may seem, I was not a fan of any of the singing cowboys. I knew that Roy Rogers and Gene Autry were both great cowboys and great Americans, and I respected them both and would always sit through their movies. But every time I would start to enjoy one of their movies, they'd start to sing to some old girl about western skies, or "I love you like a coyote loves beef." And suddenly the movie got boring.

That never happened in a Lash LaRue movie. It was fightin', shootin' and chasin' excitement all the way. They were so involved in fightin', shootin' and chasin' that sometimes they didn't even bother with a plot.

It wasn't that I minded girls in cowboy movies. They were fine as the ranchers' daughters that got rescued and the dance hall girls. I just didn't like it when they became an interruption to the Saturday afternoon violence.

John Wayne was my biggest hero, then and now. If you wanted to get me into a movie, all you had to do was put The Duke's name on a marquee. I loved his war movies and his westerns. I don't guess I ever missed a John Wayne picture, and when he died, a big chunk of my childhood was lost forevermore. John Wayne may have indeed been the last Great American hero.

BARBER SHOPS: For the most part, the barber shops of my childhood have been replaced by styling salons. I guess we are lucky to have these modern facilities, but I really miss the old barber shops.

They were easy to find because of the red-and-white striped barber pole.

Everybody had his favorite barber shop. There were four in our town, and I went to them all at one time or the other. I finally settled on my favorite and after that I never went to another.

My favorite was "Abe and Bud's." I liked it best because both Abe and Bud treated us kids like we were customers. The other shops in town treated us like we were necessary evils.

While most of their trade was adult, Abe and Bud knew every kid's name and they talked to us like we had some sense. It was much more than a place to get your hair cut; it was a great center for sports and politics.

If you really wanted the lowdown on the Atlanta Crackers, the place to get it was at Abe and Bud's. Abe could explain in great detail the Crackers' win over the Birmingham Barons, or why the New Orleans Pelicans were never gonna be a pennant contender until they decided to get a good left-handed pitcher in their bullpen.

I guess it was in Abe and Bud's barber shop that I first acquired my love of politics. I discovered that politics was just like baseball, only it took longer to play the game. From the East Point mayor's race to what old Gene Talmadge was up to at the state capitol, the answers were all available at the barber shop. All that, plus the best GI haircut around.

I can still smell that wonderful talcum powder and great hair tonic. I remember thinking that I was finally grown the first time Bud shaved the back of my neck and around my ears.

I remember how proud I was when I took my son Phil into Abe and Bud's for a haircut. I remembered how they had treated me, and they treated Phil the same.

I was glad that he got to see a real barber shop before they were all gone. I was especially proud that he became a second generation customer at Abe and Bud's.

THE POTBELLIED STOVE: Before the days of

more convenient heating, the potbellied stove was a fixture in many public places. It was made of cast iron and it burned either coal or wood.

Every small town depot and general store had one, and in the winter it became the gathering place for every old-timer in town. It was while sitting around that old stove that most of the world's problems were solved. Like most of the wonderful things of my childhood, the potbellied stove fell victim to progress. Did you ever see anybody solve a problem sitting around an automatic heater? What price progress?

THE TEN-CENT STORE: We called it the ten-cent store or the dime store, and it was a wonderful place for a childhood visit.

The name derived from the fact that in their early history they sold nothing but items priced at ten cents or less.

By the time I came along, that was not the case, but they were still a great place to go and dream.

They had wonderful candy counters where you could buy candy by the ounce. It was enough to drive you out of your little sugar-starved mind. You could get jellybeans in every shade of the rainbow. You could get candy corn or almost anything else that was pleasing to a ten-year-old palate.

The dime store was also the place to go for your school supplies. Pencils, color crayons, tablets and Blue Horse notebook paper were all waiting there to get the school year started off right.

It was also the place to prepare for any holiday. You went there to buy your mama a "Whitman Sampler" — a delicious box of candy just perfect for a Mother's Day present. On Valentine's Day, you bought her the same candy in a heart-shaped box.

Just before Halloween, you made a call on the dime store to buy your dough face, hoping against hope to buy one that nobody else already had.

On the rare occasions when I had some extra money, I would go to Carl's 5 & 10-cent store. I would wander through the toy department and look at bags of shiny, multicolored marbles. That was during the second World War, and every counter in the toy department had guns on them. There was a shortage of metal because of the war, so most of the guns were either wooden or cardboard. I didn't care. It was a great place to shop.

I would leave the toy department and head for the comic book rack. Then I would usually end up at the model airplane counter. On my way out, I spent whatever I had left at the candy counter.

The dime store was one of the sadder casualties of the march of time.

THE ICEBOX: Our icebox was very modern; it was made out of metal rather than wood. It was green and had three doors on the front. One door opened onto the compartment containing the big block of ice that Robert the Iceman brought. The other two held our perishable food.

The melting ice dripped down into a dishpan that

was on the floor beneath the icebox. It was my job to keep the dishpan emptied.

I had an enormous lack of character even in those days, so I would wait until the pan was completely full of water before I would make any attempt whatsoever to do my job.

I was then told, "Be careful. Don't spill it." When the dishpan was full, it weighed about the same thing I did. I would drag it very carefully out from under the icebox, pick it up and head for the back door. About halfway there the ice cold water would slosh up onto my little belly. I would, of course, jump like I had been shot, and water would go everywhere.

One day after witnessing one of my attempts to keep from drowning, my granddaddy said, "If you don't stop letting that dishpan get so full, boy, you're gonna be mildewed before you're fifteen years old."

It was a red letter day of joy when we finally got our first refrigerator. Anybody who misses the old icebox has never had ice cold water dumped on his belly.

THE FRONT PORCH: I'd really like to know who the first clown was that decided you could build a house without a front porch. It was a sad day when stoops started to replace front porches.

A stoop is a little old nothing stuck on the front of your house. It's just big enough for you to stand on while you're waiting for someone to open the door and let you in.

A front porch, on the other hand, was big enough to put rocking chairs on. It was also big enough to put a good old chain-squeakin' porch swing on.

The porch was a great place to sit and read the Sunday paper and wave at the cars going by. It was a great place to sit with your girlfriend and hope that her mama would turn out the porch light so that you could conduct a brief test of the girl's willpower.

It's very hard for me to imagine growing up in a world without front porches and rocking chairs. These wonderful things have been replaced by patios. It's very difficult to take any pride in a patio. That's why people put them on the back of the house, so nobody can see them.

I have high hopes that someday builders will come to their senses and start building front porches on houses again. The fireplace is back, and that gives me hope for the return of the porch.

THE OUTHOUSE: In my youth, outhouses or privies were commonplace in the rural areas. Every farmhouse had one. They are another of the things that I'm not sorry to see gone.

They were cold in the winter, hot in the summer and just not a fun place to spend any time.

There were two-holers and one-holers. I never quite understood the two-holers. I've heard of togetherness, but that's ridiculous.

I always hated using an outhouse. I know they were necessary, but I'm glad they're gone.

THE HOBOS: I've never met a hobo. As a matter of fact, I've never even seen one up close. But I always liked and admired those knights of the road.

We used to go to the railroad tracks and wait for the trains to go by to see if we could spot a hobo. When we saw one, we would all jump to our feet and start to wave like crazy as the train sped past us. The hobos always responded the same way, by waving like crazy back and yelling at us. I was always amazed at their friendliness and enthusiasm. I was sure that they were the friendliest adults on the face of the earth.

When I went to bed that night, I would think about those men and their way of life. In my young mind, it was romantic. I wanted to be a hobo. I wanted to be able to go wherever those wonderful trains would take me, with no worries about school, homework or cutting the grass. It seemed to me to be the only way to live.

What I didn't realize was that there was a depression on and that the hobos were like most people of the times — just doing their best to get by. I didn't know that those faceless men were not doing what they wanted to do, that they were doing the only thing left for them to do.

I thought their waving was a sign of friendliness. I didn't know that they weren't waving to me. They were waving to a little boy they had been forced to leave, or perhaps they were waving to the memory of a childhood that the Depression had cheated them out of.

The hobo is just one more piece of vanished America. One that I hope never comes back.

ABSOLUTE TRUTHS

In my youth, things moved a lot slower . . . or at least they seemed to. I was convinced that there were a few things in life that would never change. For example, I was just sure that —

1. Joe Louis would always be champion.
2. President Roosevelt would always lead us.
3. Johnny Weismuller would always be Tarzan, Lord of the Jungle.
4. R.C. Cola with peanuts poured in it was the ultimate treat.
5. Cherry popsicles were not fit to eat.
6. Captain Marvel could beat up Superman.
7. Both Hitler and Tojo were going to hell when they died.
8. Gene Krupa could play the drums better than anybody else.
9. Walter George and Richard Russell were the only two men allowed to be our senators.
10. Jack Armstrong really ate Wheaties.
11. Hopalong Cassidy was too old to be a real cowboy.

Ludlow Porch

12. We never would raise enough money to build the new church that Brother Boswell talked about every Sunday.

From my vantage point almost half a century later, I'm still sure of about half of these.

26

Have We Really
Given Our Kids More?

THE EXERCISE OF looking back on my childhood
has left me convinced of one thing: We grew up
slower than today's kids.

When I turned six, my mind was full of wonder
with a million questions — What will school be
like? Who will be my teacher? Will she be mean? I
hope I get that pretty yellow raincoat with the rain
hat like the policeman wears, and if I get it, I hope
it rains every day. Are we having banana pudding
for dessert tonight?

Granted, my parents may have lied to me on
occasion, but it was always an act of love. And
more times than not it was designed to preserve my
innocence.

Today by the time a kid is six he has his own
stock portfolio, wears thick glasses and has hairy
palms, and has marched in at least one anti-some-
thing-or-other parade. And the joy of innocence

213

Ludlow Porch

is long gone.

At the risk of sounding like an old grouch, I'm against it. Children are children for such a very short time, so why do their parents want to rush it?

Are all those young boys playing Little League baseball at the age of seven or eight because *they* want to or because their father wants them to? And are all those little girls cheerleaders at age eight because *they* want to be or because their mothers want them to be?

Are the parents trying to recapture their own lost childhoods through their children?

I hope someday that all parents realize the minutes of childhood go by faster than those of later life, and therefore they should be savored and enjoyed. It's OK for kids to play baseball or football without parents sitting around to ruin it for them. It's OK for children to play in sandboxes alone and with no competition.

I don't have my childhood anymore, but I do have my memories of it. And we owe at least that much to our kids.

27

It May Be Trivia, But It's Not Trivial

No BOOK OF mine about growing up would be complete without some trivia. As a matter of fact, some critics have said that my books are not complete even *with* trivia. Nonetheless, here's a few questions from the period. Whether you know the answers or not, maybe the questions will bring back some fond memories:

QUESTIONS

1. How many movies did Clark Gable and Jean Harlow make together?
2. How many times did Joe Louis defend his heavyweight crown?
3. Everyone knows the Phantom's second horse is named Hero, but can you name his first horse?
4. From the Archie comic books, can you name Jughead's dog?

5. Name the models of the Hudson automobile.
6. Who was Krazy Kat's best friend?
7. What was Tommy Dorsey's theme song?
8. Can you name the nephews of Felix the Cat?
9. How many squares are there in a hopscotch game?
10. What was the name of President Roosevelt's plane?
11. Where did Hopalong Cassidy work?
12. What was Jack Dempsey's right hand called?
13. What was Jack Teagarden's orchestra's theme song?
14. What is the shortest verse in the Bible?
15. From radio, who was Sky King's ranch foreman?
16. According to Al Capp's Lil Abner, who is the world's worst jinx?
17. Who was Pinocchio's best friend?
18. Who was Joe Palooka's manager?
19. What was Jungle Jim's last name?
20. Name Chester Riley's son.
21. How tall was King Kong?
22. What subject did "Our Miss Brooks" teach?
23. How many movies did Alan Ladd and Veronica Lake make together?
24. What song did Hank Williams have on the charts at the time of his death?
25. What was Betty Grable's nickname?
26. Where did both Blondie and Dagwood go to college?
27. Who was The Great Gildersleeve's radio nephew?

28. Who was The Lone Ranger's archenemy?
29. Who played detective Lucky Smith on radio?
30. Who is Snuffy Smith's wife?
31. From the comic books, who said, "Now I shut my eyes real tight. / Then I wish with all my might. / Magic words of poof, poof, piffles, / Make me just as small as sniffles."?
32. Name Gene Autry's horse.
33. Whose garden did Peter Rabbit invade?
34. From radio, name Gene Autry's ranch.
35. Everyone knows that Superman lives in Metropolis, but in what state is Metropolis located?
36. Who was the school teacher in the "Our Gang" comedies?
37. Name Lash LaRue's movie horse.
38. What was the theme song of the Artie Shaw Orchestra?
39. Name Roy Rogers's ranch.
40. What big band leader and TV star was the nation's youngest Eagle Scout at age thirteen?
41. What was known as the drink of Swiss mountain climbers?
42. What product was advertised as both white and blue?
43. What was "the land over the rainbow"?
44. Who was Straight Arrow's sidekick?
45. What is Mammy Yokum's first name?
46. Who is Pecos Bill's wife?
47. Name the French skunk in the Warner Brothers cartoons.

48. Name the Andrews sisters.

ANSWERS

1. Six — *The Secret Six, Red Dust, Hold Your Man, China Seas, Wife vs. Secretary, Saratoga*
2. Twenty-five
3. Thunder
4. Hot Dog
5. Commodore, Hornet, Pacemaker and Wasp
6. Ignatz Mouse
7. "I'm Getting Sentimental Over You"
8. Inky and Dinky
9. Ten
10. The Sacred Cow
11. The Bar-20 Ranch
12. Iron Mike
13. "I've Got a Right To Sing the Blues"
14. John 11:35 — "Jesus wept."
15. Jim Bell
16. Joe Btfsplk
17. Jiminy Cricket
18. Knobby Walsh
19. Bradley
20. Junior
21. Fifty feet
22. English
23. Seven
24. "I'll Never Get Out of This World Alive"
25. The Legs
26. Lehigh University

27. Leroy Forrester
28. The evil Butch Cavendish
29. Former heavyweight champion Max Baer
30. Loweezy
31. Mary Jane
32. Champion
33. Farmer McGregor
34. Melody Ranch
35. Illinois
36. Miss Crabtree, played by June Marlowe
37. Rush
38. "Nightmare"
39. The Double R Bar
40. Ozzie Nelson
41. Ovaltine
42. Rinso — "Rinso white, Rinso blue, happy little wash day song."
43. Oz
44. Packy
45. Pansy
46. Slue Foot Sue
47. Pepe Le Pew
48. Patti, Maxine and Laverne